ORAL BOOK REVIEWING TO STIMULATE READING:

A Practical Guide in Technique for Lecture and Broadcast

by

Evelyn Oppenheimer

The Scarecrow Press, Inc.
Metuchen, N.J., & London
1980

Also by Evelyn Oppenheimer:

Legend and Other Poems
The Articulate Woman: Public Speaking for Women
Red River Dust
Texas in Color
The Book of Dallas (*co-editor*)

207830

Library of Congress Cataloging in Publication Data

Oppenheimer, Evelyn, 1907-
 Oral book reviewing to stimulate reading.

 1. Book reviewing. 2. Public speaking. I. Title.
PN98.B7064   808'.066028021   80-20006
ISBN 0-8108-1352-1

*Dedicated to all the audiences who have
listened so loyally—and to the publishers
who have worked with me for so many interesting years
in our joint effort to bring more books and
readers together*

Foreword

American book publishers may point with justifiable pride to the fact that far more books are published and sold in the United States now than in any previous era. This is a healthy sign of heightening literacy and the increasing awareness of Americans to the creative and the informative rewards of book reading. However, a companion circumstance needs to be considered just as carefully. Reliable surveys have revealed that more than half of the adults in the country admit they do not read a single book within a year. Thus, in book readership, we seem to be moving toward opposite poles: increasing readership of books on the part of certain segments of the populace and expressed disinterest in books by another part.

The oral book review, delivered before gatherings of various kinds, can perform distinctive services relative to both those who already know the pleasures of book reading and those who have yet to discover books as a source of entertainment and information.

In no sense is the oral book report intended to be a substitute for reading. Rather, a review delivered with enthusiasm and clear perception should whet the appetite of the listeners and lead them to seek out the book for themselves. The non-book reader, if exposed to stimulating oral reviews, may be persuaded to move over into the ranks of the readers.

Another factor in our complex modern life adds greatly to the value of the oral book review. Today, non-fiction books supply much of the background for the problems which bewilder and plague mankind, and answers to these problems emerge through the ideas which gain expression in the printed pages. It would be impossible for the authorities who write these books to lecture in every town and city; yet it is entirely possible for the challenging ideas set forth in each of their books to be presented by an oral reviewer. Thus, the review can replace the lecture that would have been delivered by the author and become an important element in educating the public.

An oral book review, however, can be as dull as a mud-puddle. An interesting book can be transformed into a series of dull statistics: a sensitive interpretation of life through the created characters of a novel may turn into a prosaic synopsis.

Thus, we are led inevitably to recognize that anyone who would seek to deliver interesting and lively oral book reviews must give thought to the process. To such persons, Evelyn Oppenheimer's chapters of instruction will prove invaluable.

In her book Miss Oppenheimer writes interestingly about the objectives of the oral review and the various approaches by which the reviewer may recapture the spirit and the challenge of the work being reviewed. She brings to the task not only a sensitivity to creative efforts but also a natural enthusiasm which bubbles through her words. Even more important, her practical "how-to-do-it" suggestions are easy to comprehend. The oral book review seems destined to play an increasingly important function in our absorption and appreciation of the books of our times; and to Miss Oppenheimer must be given much credit for the evolution of this type of review.

DeWitt C. Reddick
Professor of Journalism Emeritus
The University of Texas
Austin, Texas

Preface

I welcome the opportunity of continuity for whatever of value this book can contribute to the oral reviewing profession in this new revised edition. After five printings of the original publication, *Book Reviewing for an Audience,* there is definite need to update many of the author and supplementary reading references previously recommended. *Tempus fugit* is the name of the game, and even as short a period of time as a decade can be an endurance test for authors and books and other media as they either pass into limbo or remain with us on the standard or classic level.

Added to this new edition is a chapter on interviewing as a supplement to the reviewer's repertoire with authors traveling hither and yon to help in the promotion of their books. It is time, too, to provide sample reviews of more recent books of note: *Roots, Sacajawea,* and *The Origin.*

The fundamentals of the reviewing technique remain the same, of course. We have the two basics to bring together—books and audiences.

The reason for this book has grown out of special courses on "Technique of the Oral Book Review and Lecture" which I have presented from 1957 through 1977 for the Adult Education Department of Texas Technological University, the Departments of Journalism and Extension at the University of Texas in Austin, the Extension Department of the University of California (Los Angeles), the Amarillo College Evening School, the Division of Special Programs of the University of Dallas, University of

Wisconsin Extension, and School of Continuing Education at Southern Methodist University.

Under the auspices of these colleges and universities, this course of professional instruction on the non-credit basis for adult education has been originated and pioneered in order to begin to supply a public demand for it. Before this, the question was repeatedly asked, "Where can I go to learn about oral book reviewing?" The answer was "Nowhere." That answer still remains the same on the undergraduate level, in spite of the need for such a course as taught by one of practical experience in the field. The undergraduate years would be ideal for this course because of the availability then of all the closely co-ordinated studies to prepare a new generation of oral reviewers.

Thirty-five years of experience and correspondence have made it evident to me that those who are interested in such practical help and instruction in oral book reviewing are in every part of our country now, and so the only way to make this information generally available is in book form.

My one most sincere hope in doing so is that there will be an ever-increasing number of women and men, young and older, who will join with me and present colleagues in developing this young profession toward its limitless future. Then we (and time) will gradually eliminate the "reviewer" who is not a reviewer at all; and then, in greater and greater numbers, books will reach the destination for which they are created and produced: the public who become fully aware of themselves and their world only in direct proportion to how much and what they read.

I gratefully acknowledge all my radio sponsors in Dallas, Houston, Phoenix, Los Angeles, San Francisco and my many sponsors on the lecture platform and in the classroom. I wish to name in addition Mallya Dean Billingsley; Dean Mary E. Miller of Southern Methodist University; and Dr. Decherd Turner, Director of Humanities Research Center, University of Texas. Most of all I am indebted to the memory of my mother and father, Gertrude and Louis Oppenheimer.

I deeply appreciate the honor of having the Foreword contributed by Dr. DeWitt C. Reddick, distinguished former

Director of the School of Journalism at University of Texas, now Professor Emeritus, who always taught the highest standards and broadest aspects of his subject.

EVELYN OPPENHEIMER

Dallas, Texas

Contents

chapter I

History of the Profession

Reviewing books is almost as old a profession as the art of writing them, though for a good many years it was termed Literary Criticism.

The Golden Age of that period was in the eighteenth and the nineteenth centuries and even very early in the twentieth. Then editors were less harried by advertising managers, and critics were given space for essays on books and authors. Also, there was a public with both the interest and the time to read what one respected mind had to say about another.

Space became less, and the critical essay became a book review relegated to a back page or column.

But, inevitably, a new form evolved to supplement the printed review and to reach a much broader audience. This was the oral review, first given from the lecture platform and then later via the microphone on radio.

The book review-lecture began to appear in the late 1920's. The most interesting fact connected with its evolution was that, contrary to the history and tradition of most cultural developments in America, the point of origin was not in the East but on the West Coast. The oral book review began in California (the Los Angeles area) and its popularity moved next to the Southwest. It appeared and flourished in Texas, then Oklahoma, and eastward through the Midwest.

Why? This was something new, and the new began coming from a younger part of the country—a society generating its own

1

entertainment. The depression years of the 1930's had a fringe benefit of their own that was little realized at the time. Men and women turned, or returned, to the basis of personal entertainment; they stayed at home and read.

Our literature itself had a new excitement and attraction. World War I had produced a generation of writers who had plenty to say and a different way of saying it. Realism had emerged, for better or worse. There was nothing new about realism, but it was new in the twentieth century. There was a great deal to think and talk about concerning what Hemingway, Remarque, Steinbeck, Sandburg, and Lewis were writing and the way they were writing. In non-fiction the reports of men like Shirer began appearing. The reaction to one war was hardly expressed before another was taking shape. People read.

There was much of transition to learn, and it could be done in the most satisfactory and entertaining way for the individual, as always, through books. In fact the same is true today, despite television, as journalism has invaded literature with political reporting in book form; in fiction the espionage novel has become a major resource in the mystery-suspense field.

The lecture platform was dead and deadly. Agencies had sent out too many celebrities with nothing to say and no ability as speakers. European "names" had come over to tell America what was wrong with us from what they had learned on brief visits at the Waldorf.

The clubwomen of America took over and came up with something new—at least a hybrid that looked new. They called it the "book review." Sometimes it was.

No group has been more ridiculed and caricatured than the clubwomen, yet no group has contributed more vitality and variety to the cultural scene in this country. They have rushed in where no angel would dare put foot or wing. They have prodded and pushed men into action for civic causes from the wilderness community level on to the metropolitan.

But it was when they wanted and needed a new type of program to entertain themselves that they began the oral book review.

It would not be illogical to assume that an impetus came

from the man whose weekly radio broadcasts as The Town Crier frequently featured his own enthusiasm for certain new books—the late Alexander Woollcott. Undoubtedly he would be aghast at having this responsibility laid at his door, but even his rotund ghost can surely stand the shock by now.

Reviewing and discussing new books revived the lost lure of the lecture, even though these programs were not called lectures. They still are not billed that way. The word "lecture" had become too formidable; "review" sounded lively, current, informal, individual.

I doubt that as many sins were ever committed under one name, for there were several flies in this new ointment. The ladies wanted to be informed, but they also expected to be entertained. Who was to do it?

The person who had reviewing experience on a paper could be inarticulate or inaudible as a speaker. He could also be quite a bore. Professors of so-called modern literature courses had all the limitations of a course of study that most often ended with poor old Silas Lapham. Persons without any reviewing experience or literary background could put on quite a show with all the folderol of old-time elocution, and often did. Worse yet, they still do.

To be sure, there had been serious study clubs led by able members all over the country. To the urban sophisticate it still comes as a surprise to hear that there are Browning, Brontë, and Shakespeare clubs in small towns in what is referred to as "the sticks." They exist and they function, shedding their light monthly on groups that may have only several dozen members.

But to review a current book was a pioneer project in city or small town clubs. There was no pattern, no precedent. The reviewers literally had to play it by ear.

I recall that when I returned to Dallas from the University of Chicago, the local chapter of the Council of Jewish Women asked me to "give a book review" for an audience of several hundred members and guests. That was early in the 1930's, and they wanted no less than Eugene O'Neill's "Mourning Becomes Electra."

I had been writing reviews for that splendid page which

Llewellyn Jones edited for what was then the *Chicago Post,* but I had never heard of "giving" one, orally.

Interested at once in anything concerning books, I went to work on what I thought such a thing should be. The results were even more interesting. It seemed that I had done something different. There were those who violently liked my review and those who strongly disliked it. The latter were of more interest to me.

In order to hear and judge what was being done, I managed to get invited to a number of other review programs. They were all presented at private clubs and organizations of social and church groups. I was horrified, to put it mildly, by what I heard. There was one exception—the outstanding work of a former schoolteacher, the late Mrs. Roscoe Bates. Otherwise, there was nothing but storytelling, no reviewing in any sense of the word. Frustrated actresses of amateur stature were having a field day.

That was when the missionary zeal hit me personally and professionally.

Here was the biggest opportunity, the greatest potential for a new *popular* development in book reviewing. A young profession was taking shape, however awkwardly, which could be far more effective than its old parent in print.

The element of personal contact with an audience was all-important. The factor of public interest opened a vista of programs far beyond the confines of private clubs and far beyond the minority who read the written review. The result could be the most influential stimulus to book reading ever exerted.

In the winter of 1936 I opened the first public oral book review series of programs in the United States. A Dallas department store with an auditorium seating 500 (later enlarged to 800 capacity) was the sponsor. The original plan called for a program once a month. Instead, the schedule came to be once a week by popular demand.

The first book featured on that series was Santayana's "The Last Puritan." Before the summer hiatus, I introduced a first novel by an unknown author whom I considered to have a major new talent in narrative technique. At the time, most reviewers of the press looked down their noses at the book. The title was "Gone with the Wind."*

---

*Original review included in Chapter 10.

chapter 2

Distinctions of the Oral Review
from the Written Review

From my experience in both fields of the reviewing profession (oral and written), I have found that there are definite
distinctions to be learned and followed. These are the differences
of media and of what people absorb through the eye and through
the ear. Such practicalities as space for the former and time for
the latter are also very much involved.

The reviewer who writes for a paper or a magazine should be
reviewing all the books that come to his desk or assigning them to
be reviewed. These reviews should appear as soon after the
publication release date set by the publisher as possible. Obviously, the review that appears three or six months after a book has
come out will not be of much publicity benefit in launching it and
calling readers' attention to it. A slip or a card giving the release
date is enclosed in all advance review copies for this reason.

The written review, the technique of which is not our
concern in this book, has as much or as little leeway as the editor
allows. It can be a page or any fraction of a column. It can, if
desired, do nothing but express the reviewer's poor opinion of the
book, his contempt and ridicule.

The oral review cannot do this. If it did, it would make anything
but good listening, especially to those in the audience who have
not yet read the book under discussion and who are always in the
majority. The oral reviewer expresses all-out negative criticism in
an entirely different manner as you will see in Chapter 5. This

5

method is even more emphatic because it can and does simply eliminate the book by overt rejection. Otherwise, prolonged criticism of a book can boomerang. It can produce the opposite effect by making people want to rush out and get the book in order to see how bad it really is. I learned this a good many years ago when I spent a 15-minute radio review broadcast pointing out what second-rate work a first-rate writer can produce (Steinbeck's "Wayward Bus"). The next day the manager of a local bookstore called to express his thanks. The publicity was selling out his stock of the title.

It must be remembered, too, that the eye can take in much more than the ear. A written review can be read in whole or in part; it can be put down and then returned to at a later time. The oral review demands more concentration from the listener. Therefore it must be presented in a way that does its entire job and achieves its dual purpose (for the book and for the audience) within a time limit as brief as possible. Why?—because aural concentration is tiring. When a listener says, "I could listen to you for hours," consider yourself complimented, of course, but don't take it seriously! Leave the filibuster to the legislators.

chapter 3

Purposes of the Oral Review

The purpose always to be kept in mind by the oral reviewer is a double-headed one. This can be illustrated best by the fact that you know it's "mission accomplished" when a listener says one of two things to you after a program: either "Now I want to read that book" or "Now I understand the book better than when I read it." Nothing else matters except these two audience reactions.

If someone fawns upon you after a program with compliments about your charm and appearance and declares that "now I won't need to read the book—your review was so wonderful," consider yourself damned as a complete failure. You have not reviewed the book at all. You have killed it.

The primary function of the oral reviewer is to stimulate reader interest and to offer his interpretation of a book. This two-in-one job comprises the alpha and omega of your work.

As a reviewer in any professional sense of the word, you are also a subtle salesman for the book as you evaluate it. If you ask an audience how many have read any current book which you are to review, you will always find that the majority have not yet read it. If this were not so, your technique would be entirely different, for then you could assume a knowledge on their part that would make it possible to concentrate on critical discussion. This, however, is not a situation that you will often encounter in any public audience.

Therefore, you must be equally entertaining and interesting

to both that majority who are the potential readers and the minority who already know the book. You must have something of value to give to each group.

You must remember that even those who have read the book all too often have read only a digest or an abridgment. In some cases, where books have been overwritten and poor editing has not removed the padding, such condensations are not abortive. But, in most cases of good writing, this popular surgery contributes to rather than cures a major social ailment.

That illness of our time is what might be called the "jet-propelled mind"; its chief symptom is an obsession for speed. This haste to get and swallow everything in capsule form—this sense of endless pressure as carried over into our cultural life—is not only farcical but fatal. No time is allowed for any thoughtful digestion or meditation about what is read. Readers settle for just a "shot" of an author's ideas and then trust that this injection will circulate through their mental blood stream.

When this does not work, they turn to a specialist, a so-called expert, an analyst: the reviewer. Of course this is good for the reviewing profession, but it imposes no little responsibility since you are working with people who are out of the habit of thinking for themselves.

A generation has come up who are *listeners* and *lookers* rather than thinkers. The radio and the television screen have conditioned this. Yet, the fact remains that these media find their source of material of any quality in the permanence of the written word. However, a book not only implies but also requires a participation in the author's thought. It is not a spectator sport. The reader carries the ball. The author throws it. The reviewer runs the interference that opens the field.

As opposed to the academic critic, the reviewer is committed to the public. We know that the public taste is just as good as it is bad. Any study of best-seller lists back through the years is proof of this. Always there is the same variety of interests on every level of public taste. This variety in itself shows a healthy resistance to the cults imposed by critics. To deplore the public taste is as bad as trying to exploit it.

This view is directly opposed to that expressed by many who

tend the flame of their own little campfire and for self-preservation contend that only the critics (themselves, of course) can recognize literature and preserve it in the jars they label and store away. Now it is true that specialists are required to label jars, but the tasting of their contents is for everyone who has an appetite and a palate.

Besides, if writers wrote only for academic critics, the publishers and the booksellers would have been out of business long ago. As a critic, I rise to the defense of the public. Guidance they need, yes, but not from the mole-hill of holier-than-thou snobbery.

After all, the people made Shakespeare, just as in our own time they have put writers on the best-seller list who have given them the self-expression (or self-delusion) which they want and need. The Babbitts and the Main Streeters themselves made Sinclair Lewis, and the men and women who have come to live with challenge responded to Hemingway.

In most cases, the public does not care who writes a book and seldom remembers the author's name, as any librarian or bookseller will tell you. But when a writer is heavily promoted for one reason or another, as was done with Pasternak and his "Dr. Zhivago" or Solzhenitsyn and "Gulag Archipelago," people become temporarily self-conscious about the social need to make at least a casual literary acquaintance with what is the vogue. However, when an author has established a real popularity, then his or her name attracts a steady following of readers, as have, for example, Irving Stone, Leon Uris, Chaim Potok, Norah Lofts, James Michener, Saul Bellow, John Updike, John Cheever, Kurt Vonnegut, Mary Stewart, Victoria Holt, Bernard Malamud, Howard Fast, Morris West, Louis Auchincloss, and Barbara Tuchman, to name a variety.

Whether an author be known or unknown, the oral reviewer's purpose remains clearly defined: to stimulate ever-increasing reader interest and to open doors to interpretation that otherwise would be passed by.

But that is not all, for whenever you are working with the spoken word, entertainment is involved. At least it should be. Anything educational never fails to be enhanced by being presented entertainingly. We can all only wish that more teachers realized this fact. The few who do are the ones we remember.

To be entertaining obviously does not mean turning handsprings or competing with comedians. But there is no reason on earth for presenting any subject without injecting some flair and *esprit* into it. Certainly, when you stand before an audience, however large or small, it's desirable to make that time enjoyable and memorable, not with tricks but by your own vitality and personality. To combine education and entertainment is "an end devoutly to be wished." To ridicule this as "sugar coating" is often only the defense of those who cannot do it.

Finally, these multiple purposes of oral reviewing conclude with the need to *evaluate* the book under discussion. Has the author accomplished what he set out to do? How does the book compare with others in the same field and/or with the author's other work? Is there relation between style and subject?

If and when you have made your listeners want to read the book, served as a springboard toward its interpretation, and performed the function of adding your contribution toward adult education in current literature according to the best of your knowledge and judgment of relative literary values which you have imparted concerning that book—when and if you have done all this in the most entertaining way possible, then it can be said that you have fulfilled the purposes of professional oral reviewing.

Not every audience wants this. Some want a story-telling hour or a dramatic reading. They don't read and they don't want to be made to have such a disturbing desire. Therefore, have no regrets if that type of audience is lost to you. Book reviewing is one thing, and other things are, obviously, other things.

However, there is a most legitimate and highly professional group who have a specific need for an exception to these rules. This exception is rightly called a "book report" or "evaluation," and the group comprises the men and women who staff the thousands of libraries throughout the United States. In most cases, they have a system of departmental meetings (adult, juvenile, etc.) at regular intervals for the purpose of reporting on new books which have been assigned to them or chosen by them for individual reading. In this way they inform each other about the books. The purpose is entirely informational.

This situation, therefore, definitely requires a process of briefing, of presenting the content of a book in highly condensed form. A personal reader reaction or critical evaluation is also desired in order to decide whether or not the book should be stocked, and, if so, in what quantity. Completely contrary to reviewing, the purpose here is to offer and supply a substitute for reading in order to save the reading time of other members of the staff. Only for such a closed group and such functional reason is it valid to give the complete core of a book and to acquaint persons with it vicariously. Even so, the projection of pro or con enthusiasm certainly adds some welcome spark and flair to the routine of this ersatz procedure.

I have attended such library meetings, and it would be an excellent idea if more reviewers were to do so—especially in the larger cities, where the libraries have multiple branches as well as departmental heads. When a reviewer sees and hears the dependence of librarians on the reliability of reviews and the way they are referred to, it generates a new sense of responsibility. Of interest, too, is the demonstrated ability of many librarians to highlight and "nutshell" the content of a book. In fact, if they are able to develop the technique of expansion of their material and original commentary, they can be a source of excellent oral reviewers.

It should be borne in mind by the librarian who goes before the public that reviewing a book is not to be confused with reporting on and surveying a number of books. Such a survey has its place, of course, at certain times and with certain groups who want a cafeteria assortment of books of various types presented in order to get an idea of what appeals to them, or for their children, or for gift-giving. But in these "book talks" there is the danger of degenerating into what can amount to little more than a hodge-podge assembly of jacket blurbs. Remember, too, that a cafeteria has organization; the vegetables are not mixed up with the desserts. In like manner, books should be grouped and related according to type, subject, and theme (contemporary novels, historical novels, travel, for example). Otherwise, unless he is taking notes, a listener finds it difficult to remember which title is about what.

At its best, a book review is devoted to one book. If more are to be presented, keep the number at a minimum so that you can be as thorough as time permits and do justice to each one. The quality of your reviews will be more effective in stimulating reader interest than the quantity of books you manage to squeeze into a given review.

The only other special cases which of necessity alter the book review purposes are the book reports of students in school or college. These reports, of course, must be very detailed in order to make it evident to teachers that the book has really been read.

Book programs for organized audiences of the blind, such as the Lighthouse groups, also demand a special treatment which requires a more detailed presentation of any book's content than would be done under normal conditions.

chapter 4

Educational Background
and Approach

Of course you like to read or you would not be interested in book reviewing, but as a reviewer, reading becomes more than a pleasure. It is also your study and your work.

Feeling the "call" as in certain other fields is not enough for a reviewer. First and forever you read, for, no matter how much you have read, it is only a shimmer on a drop in the Niagara of world literature. All that one has to do is to walk into the entrance of our own Congressional Library to sense the overwhelming awe of all that man has recorded in writing and the infinitesimal percentage which one individual can hope to absorb in one short lifetime. But this is challenge, not frustration.

First of all, get balance in your reading. For every two or three new books that you read, read an older book of standard literature, so that you add to your knowledge of earlier writers. It may be that you turn back to classics which you missed along the way or were forced to read before you were ready either to enjoy or to understand them. It may be that you become acquainted with modern authors preceding those of today—Cather, Wharton, Mann, Wolfe, Bromfield, Galsworthy, Sinclair, James, Cabell, Maurois, Lewis, Wister, Dreiser, Maugham, Anderson, France, Shaw, to name only a few. And of course the poets: Millay, Lowell, Robinson, Teasdale, Brooke, Lawrence, Lindsay, Frost, Masters, Sandburg. Such background is necessary to highlight the material of interest and concern today. It enriches

your own approach to what is being written now and enables you
to point out and refer to differences or developments which can
add insight and perspective to the book you are reviewing.

However, books themselves are not enough for this background. It is just as necessary to be as well-informed as possible
on current events and also other current reviews and book news
in general. Although many people depend on radio and television
for news and commentary, the majority still follow a local paper.
So should you. Then, too, many papers include a Sunday book
review page or at least a column. In addition, you should read
fairly regularly a national paper such as the *New York Times,* the
Christian Science Monitor, or the *Wall Street Journal.*

The *New York Times* has a Sunday book review section which
can be subscribed to independently at very nominal cost; on the
whole, coverage is reasonably good and not too cultist.

Most women students are usually surprised at my recommendation to read the *Wall Street Journal.* Many of them still seem
to think that it is exclusively financial in content and therefore
incomprehensible, for some strange reason. However, the *Wall
Street Journal* has some of the finest book reviewing in this country
on its editorial page under the headings "The Bookshelf" and
"Reading for Pleasure."

One of the weekly news magazines, such as *Time* or *News-
week,* should also be on your list, but it can be borne in mind that
often these book reviews may be slanted to follow the editorial
policies of these magazines. In such cases, when tongue-in-cheek
swells out to look like the mumps, observe the proper quarantine
protection. Remember that a wisecrack only shows the crack in a
person's wisdom. It can get a laugh, but seldom a reader. It has
pepper, but no salt. Too often they are also cultist.

None of these top-ranking printed media should be regarded
as sanctified gospel. They are aids to be used with a proper sense
of the way their values vary. It is not uncommon to see slipshod
work, superficiality, and lack of objectivity in these reviews. It is
not at all impossible, at times, to discern evidence of reviewers
who have limited their reading to the jacket covers and the
publishers' promotion sheets. Why keep up with these magazines, then? They are necessary because many fine reviews do

appear, and these contacts enlarge and expand your own thinking as a reviewer.

Naturally, everyone's time is limited, and we cannot sit with our eyes eternally glued to the printed word. But a reviewer of any distinction must read as much and as widely as possible. He or she must be informed both within and without the literary field, for all current events feed your interpretation of books which are contemporary in subject. In fact, even in reviewing a historical novel or a biography, your knowledge and mention of a current event can often point out a parallel that adds present interest to the past and makes an audience aware of the way in which history repeats itself.

Time for reading as much as we should is not our only problem. Cost is another obstacle to surmount. How can you afford all these books and papers and magazines? There are public libraries. There are paper-back reissues of both classic and modern authors. There is, finally, always a way to manage and sacrifice one thing for another, if that other is more important to you.

For the reviewer, a publication such as *Publishers Weekly* or *Library Journal* is an important source of book news and advance announcements. These two magazines may not be "musts," but they are a definite help to the reviewer.

A real necessity in your background information is biographical material on the authors of the books you review. A brief and accurate résumé of the writer's life is always a vital part of the book review. This résumé is an educational feature of interest to the majority of your audience. It also serves as a refresher to those who have only a vague knowledge about the author. People like to know about people.

Getting this information is not at all difficult. In the case of the classic and early modern authors, a visit to any public library will yield more than enough material for your needs. This is also true of major contemporary writers. On your own, you can get good biographical dictionaries which should be part of your private reference library anyway. "Webster's Biographical Dictionary" is available in updated editions and you can check on others at the bookstore and library.

Of course, most books have biographical sketches of their authors on the jacket cover, or at the end of the book, or sometimes within Prefaces and Introductions. These can be adequate or inadequate. If no biographical material appears in the book, there is one thing you can always do easily at the cost of a postage stamp. If you are not on a publisher's mailing list as a professional reviewer, write the publicity director of that company and ask for biographical material on any author whom they publish. You will receive it, for publishers maintain departments of advertising, publicity, and promotion to supply such material. In this connection may I suggest that when you ask for something, however free and readily available, it is always professional as well as good manners to identify yourself. This can be done by naming a reference (a local bookstore or librarian) or by enclosing a press clipping concerning you as a reviewer. This is not necessary, but it is good professional policy and will help you to establish yourself on the records of the publishing company.

Is all of this too much to do? No, it is not. Yet, oral book reviewing is more demanding of your time than some professions. It can never be done as thoroughly and perfectly as you wish, because the presentation required is constantly dynamic.

In an article entitled "The Journalism of Book Reviewing," Granville Hicks wrote that "In spite of the widespread belief that any halfway literate person can write a book review, the truth is that book reviewing is a difficult art." Amen to that. This applies even more strongly to the oral review which requires both the written and the spoken word, and therefore an additional technique. This being the case, a person may have the inclination, the desire, and the talent; but these essentials are not enough by themselves. There must be education—not necessarily a product of degrees, but an informed background. There must be discipline, trained or self-taught or self-imposed—an awareness of purpose and responsibility.

Otherwise, how can a man or woman be equipped, however well endowed, to do justice to literary work of any magnitude and originality, much less to have anything of value to say about it that would arouse reader interest in audiences? In order to convey a book's values, one must first know something about literary values in general. Acquiring and developing that knowledge is a reviewer's never-ending preparation.

chapter 5

Selection of Books to Review

In oral reviewing, you perform your first function as a critic by selecting the books you will review. This selective process, as we have said, is a major distinction of the oral review. The books you eliminate in spite of any popular or promotional pressure are, for various reasons, the index of your standards as a critic in this field of reviewing. In this way, as in so many others, professional integrity can be known just as well by what is *not* done as by what is. What seems negative is the result of very positive thinking.

In many cases, your rejection of a book does not mean that the book is second-rate or in anyway sub-standard in quality. You eliminate it simply because it does not lend itself to the purposes of oral reviewing. In other cases, of course, you exclude a book for definitely critical reasons. It may be because of blatant inaccuracies in the case of biography or the historical and biographical novel. We have more than enough misinformation in society, unfortunately, without adding to it by recommending books by writers who are deliberately misleading or careless in their research. This has to be watched especially with books set in the Biblical period, for in them, readers all too often look not for facts but merely for what will reinforce their prejudices and adorn their ignorance.

Obviously, if a book is poorly written and on a publisher's list for reasons known only to himself in his darkest moments, or is cheap in content and lacking any *raison d'être,* you should not waste your own or an audience's time with it.

No doubt the question most probably forming in your mind is "But how do you get out of reviewing a book which they ask you to do?" The answer is very simple: you refuse. You do it gracefully, of course, and you state your reason or reasons. Naturally, you express your regret at not being able to comply with this request. Point out that the book does not measure up to the standards you know are theirs. This psychology is usually effective, because hardly anyone wants to question his own standards. By all means then, suggest another choice of books, recommending several. In most cases, you will find the willingness to make a change, and the better your review the more they will wonder why any other title was even considered.

If, however, this does not work and the book under fire is still insisted on, stand by your guns. You are sorry, but that particular book is not on your list for the reason or reasons given. Let them get someone else to do it. The loss of one engagement will not bankrupt you. Keep your professional integrity intact. After all, what else do you have?

At times, there are other and more insidious kinds of pressure brought to bear on professional reviewers. One is by the author who happens to be a personal friend, or "a friend of a friend," or, worse yet, a relative. He or she assumes that you simply must review his or her book; not to do so would be to behave like a cad and prove that you don't appreciate literary art when you see it.

If the book is poor, you have no choice. You prove yourself a cad; you do not review it. One person's or one family's resentment is preferable to the loss of professional respect. There are many ways of saying "no" with grace and finesse. If, for example, you operate on a schedule (as most of us do), you can say that your schedule is filled or perhaps you can explain that you happen not to have the proper audience for that type of book. There is always a way to avoid blunt unkindness, and, despite the fact that many writers say that they want the truth from an editor or a reviewer, pleasant or unpleasant, very few can take it when they get the latter. Human nature just happens to be like that.

When the book in question is a good one, you review it of course. Even so, still another problem is present. It is absolutely necessary to divorce yourself from your personal relationship with the author in order to do a good job. Otherwise, the audience can get the idea that the book is secondary to that relationship, and the book gets lost among the bouquets presented too personally and not objectively enough. No tendency is more natural than to favor one's friends, but, as a reviewer, your best friends are good books and the people who read them.

The other pressure put on reviewers is direct or indirect bribery. This can occur when a publisher or an author contrives to get a reviewer obligated to him through some personal favor, aid, gifts, or entertainment in order to obtain "good reviews." Sometimes it works the other way around through the press when a newspaper or a magazine bargains with a publisher for advertisements in exchange for "good review space." Fortunately, such deplorable dealings sooner or later become known, and usually sooner than is thought.

If, in your judgment of local conditions, a book is too controversial with regard to religion, politics, or sociology for any intelligent approach, appreciation, and response to it, don't force the issue. This is not a matter of cowardice, but one of practical common sense. To be provocative is one thing and highly desirable; to arouse resentment and resistance to an author will help neither his cause nor his sales. One exception to this is controversy on the sex content of a book, for the public invariably wants to read what "they say" should not be read.

Any book's subject, however controversial, can be reviewed with the proper know-how and handling—but not by the beginner. Waving a red flag before a bull should follow some experience with *el toro* in the ring.

You select your books, first of all, for their literary value. They must be good in the basic sense of good writing. We do not wait for great writing or we would be among the unemployed. When "great" writing emerges, so does a question at times. Is writing great which excites and satisfies several hundred critics or hundreds of thousands of readers? The wise reviewer does not answer that question for at least 50 years, and by then he or she retires in order to give it more thought.

As an oral reviewer, you also make your selection of books

for entertainment value. Here the word "entertainment" is used in its widest, most fundamental sense of holding attention and interest. Unless you are speaking to an especially selected audience or a closed circuit, you would not review a book on a subject without some potential of general appeal.

Always mindful of your double purpose of stimulating reader interest and furthering interpretation, select books which provide original discussion material: something to think about, something to talk about.

This excludes the purely plot novel. It is a fine form for good reading, but it is not for oral reviewing. When the accent is entirely on plot, the review becomes mere story-telling, and the sale of the book in that audience, except for gift purchases, is finished. In addition, the novel written for plot alone requires no interpretation.

Very often, though, a novel which seems to rely only on plot does not really do so. Daphne du Maurier's "Rebecca" is an excellent example. Apparently it is all plot and suspense—but is it? Actually, the essence and impact are its character studies, and the story does not matter half so much as the characters because the story comes from them. What is memorable and meaningful are a man, his second wife, a housekeeper, and the omnipresent spirit of the first wife. Here is all the drama of human nature, its good and its evil. This could be brought out in a review, to give the audience a fuller appreciation of a remarkable technique.

Characterization is a major factor in the selection of books for oral review. The analysis of human beings, their actions, thoughts, and feelings, gives you endless material to discuss in relation to the ways in which writers use it and reveal it. Every good novelist and biographer offers another revelation of the mystery of human nature which forever confronts and fascinates us all. People are, after all, the greatest of all subjects in literature, and the how and the why of the way we act and react within ourselves and to each other is not only our chief entertainment but also the biggest challenge to our understanding.

Long before psychology came to be considered a possible science, the novelist and the dramatist and the poet had explored every facet of the subject. They were our first psychologists, and the great authors of both the past and the present remain our best explorers of inner space.

A word of caution should be injected here for the beginner. Do not select a novel of too many characters, for in trying to present all of them you will only confuse your audience. Later in your experience you will be more able to distinguish between major and minor characters in a densely populated novel.

A classic example of a limited cast of perfectly defined characters which I have always recommended to my students is the Edith Wharton novelette, "Ethan Frome" (see Chapter 10 for review). In it are only three major characters, but, even so, most beginners invariably include minor ones in their reviews.

Other outstanding and later examples of fiction of very few and strongly delineated characters are Hemingway's "Old Man and the Sea" (see Chapter 10) Chaim Potok's "My Name Is Asher Lev" (see Chapter 10), and Wallace Stegner's "The Spectator Bird."

Still another major source of books for oral reviewing is the book which was written as an expression of an idea, a message, or a philosophy. Here again there is mental meat for digestion and discussion.

Novels, memoirs, autobiographies, plays and books dealing with world affairs, current events, history, philosophy, as well as inspirational and self-help books—all have come to lay heavy emphasis on some specific angle. World wars, world changes and conflicts in politics, economics, and customs, have generated a vast amount of writing. Men and women seek outlets for their ideas and causes. They write not so much in order to create as to influence and convert or to alert and arouse. They are either missionaries or Paul Reveres.

This type of book, whatever its form, imposes a special responsibility, for it requires more than the usual objectivity on your part. You are to review it, not re-write it or distort it. You must distinguish and point out the difference between bias and sincerity; otherwise, you only add to confused thinking.

Another type of book which offers great attraction and also presents a problem, especially for the beginner in reviewing, is the one whose distinction rests on the author's literary style. Usually, this is a novel written to express and project a mood or atmosphere through fine, often beautiful writing. Unfortunately, we do not get many of these. Richard Llewellyn's Welsh novels, "How Green Was My Valley" and "Up, Into the Singing Mountain" are examples of this. Marjorie Rawlings, author of "The Yearling," and Fred Gipson were writers of this school (see Chapter 10 for a review of Gipson's "Hound-Dog Man") as was Margaret Cravens in her "I Heard the Owl Call My Name."

Regional writers usually convey a poetic sensitivity to the primitive and match it with a style which reflects that quality. Their stories are shaped by the settings. Scene and sound are dominant, and it is difficult for the reviewer to describe this adequately and effectively except through direct quotations.

You might ask here, "But what about the Hemingway style?" That is something different, for his is a style of characterization. Moreover, in a Hemingway story the accent is on characters and thought, not the rhythm of time and place, not even in "Old Man and the Sea."

There is, however, one other case where style per se is most important. That is poetry.

Nothing has been more regrettable on our literary scene in America during this century than the small quantity and still smaller quality of poetry from the publishers. This does not mean that good poetry is not being written. Poetry, good and bad, is always being written, for the poet is one of nature's most direct instruments of expression.

The present, and we hope temporary, situation is that during a time when people are in a state of emotional reaction to great changes in the world, the movement to match those changes with new and experimental forms captures the attention of critics and editors. When the public fails to respond, a false conclusion is drawn that "there's no interest in poetry." What really happens is that the *public* clings to the traditional. They continue to want what they have always wanted from poetry—beauty, the essence of thought, solace, inspiration, the reality of romance. These are the "quotes" that they turn and return to when moments of great joy and great sorrow overwhelm them.

Except for biographies or biographical novels about poets,

new collections and anthologies, and special event programs, there is less reviewing of poetry than of any other literary form. But whenever there is opportunity (or you can make an opportunity occur), the only way to review poetry is to quote as many excerpts as needed in order to have the audience come into direct contact with the poet. *This method applies only to poetry*. The biographical introduction of the writer, the commentary of interpretation and evaluation, will remain integral parts of your review as in the case of any other form.

In reviewing a play, your technique is to be just the same as it would be with any other work of fiction. You are *not* to give a reading. If you do that, it is a reading, not a review. In addition you are usually violating the copyright which in the published play expressly forbids such readings without official permission. We are all well aware that officials cannot be running around the country to check up on every Mrs. John Doe who is gaily competing with Broadway. But our interest in the matter is not a legal one but a professional one. We rise to protest only when she calls her performance a review.

A play, like a novel, has setting, characters, plot. Its form, in print, calls for no different approach in reviewing. Naturally, the ability to visualize it in performance and to suggest those effects *in your own words* can be of great benefit. Inevitably, too, there may be quotation of a few lines to highlight a character or a situation, but this must be held to a minimum.

Even a musical such as "The King and I" could be reviewed with the same technique as its original source, "Anna and the King of Siam." Each told the same story with equal potency of character study and message of tolerance and understanding (see Chapter 10).

One more factor remains to be considered in the selection of books for oral reviewing, and that is suitability of the book to the audience. This calls for a judgment of people, and often this can be more difficult than a judgment of books.

There was a time when it would have been poor judgment to feature a highly sophisticated book for anything but a metropolitan audience. This is certainly no longer so. Travel and communication now have made the so-called small-town audience no different from any other.

Most people everywhere want and respond to the same things: human interest, an entertainment angle, and some new information or thought to take home with them. This you will find to be so with both men and women. True, men generally have more interest in the factual material of non-fiction and the historical novel, but contemporary fiction of top quality or on topical subjects holds great appeal for them.

Certainly this is so with recent and current novels concerning political life, the form that Allen Drury began in "Advise and Consent" in 1959 and which has spawned through dozens of journalists who have turned to narrative reporting in non-fiction books, such as those by Thomas Thompson and the Larry Collins and Dominique LaPierre team. Books of commentary and analysis on exposures of scandals like Watergate, plus the memoirs of men and women involved in events of such controversy, must be reviewed in the context of those events with allowance made for the writer's personal bias and the fact that it takes time for history to be fairly assessed, longer even than many historians realize. Certainly the news media reporters and commentators reflect an environment not conducive to producing books of perspective. Beware of instant analysis. A notable exception was the high quality of the in-depth work of William Shirer.

There was a time, too, when women assumed that they could be interested only in novels, but gradually reviewers have introduced them to the fact that biography, autobiography, memoirs, etc., are just as fascinating as the novel. Modern women are aware that, as voters, workers, and investors, they need all available reading of current events analysis just as vitally and as urgently as do men.

The difference in reading tastes and interests between the sexes no longer poses any problem. The "mixed" audience is only somewhat difficult when the mixing is with age groups, such as adults and high school boys and girls. Often these students have been lured to the program to make a "report" and for the extra credit promised by their teachers. Actually, it's a fine idea, but they come with a do-or-die attitude, and at any mention of sex they dissolve into giggles and wiggles. Usually, if you ignore this, it stops. If not, and you see that the rest of the audience is being disturbed, just interrupt yourself a moment to remark that you had assumed that this was an adult audience. Since the teen-ager hates to be considered childish or in any way lacking in sophistication, your troubles are over.

The point is, as we shall stress later, never to "talk down" from one level to another. If you do, the upper level is aware of it, is insulted and bored. If you don't, the lower level rises to meet the compliment and challenge. Talking down is not only as bad as showing off, it is also a form of it.

You will encounter regional differences of interest and, unfortunately, prejudice which can make certain books especially suitable or unsuitable. It would, for instance, be courting some personal danger as well as a total lack of reader interest to review a biography of General Sherman in any town along his line of march.

Very often a program committee chairman will confide that her club, organization, or convention wants "something light— good, but not heavy—and not too spicy for our older members— just something light." They know what they want or at least they know what they don't want, and so must you. Do not worry if at night you begin dreaming of a literary electronic scale, down on one side with the "heavyweight" books and up on the other with the "lightweights." This is the image which booksellers also report after days of receiving such orders.

Just remember that there are more than enough books in every category for every taste in every season, and books with the light touch of humor in characterization, situation, thought and commentary can be of very high quality. Humorists are all too few in our time, alas, but Dorothy Gilman has done some very good comic novelettes; in the memoir form, Sam Levenson has been prodigious with his concentrates of wisdom about human nature. Jean Kerr and Erma Bombeck have provided their wit. If indeed the pen is mightier than the sword, it need not be a sledgehammer to impress a truth. A needle can do it, too, and often far more effectively, for its power is in the skill of the hand that uses it.

Bear in mind, however, that all people do not react to the same kinds or levels of humor. Farce can become too broad, and satire too sharp and sophisticated, and of course poor taste is always poor taste. Yours is not a television studio audience assembled to be directed by signs and signals to laugh on cue. Yours is a *thinking* audience comprised of people who want to be entertained, yes, but with *your* sense of *their* responsiveness.

No category of books has become more popular than the self-help variety. Dale Carnegie started it all with his bestseller of 1936, "How to Win Friends and Influence People." Since then, the public demand reflecting a need for books to bolster confidence and to cope with this twentieth century, as well as to be happy, healthy, sexy, wealthy, and wise has been a publishing bonanza. Such books are to be chosen for reviewing with the most special care for their validity and quality, as for example, Dr. David Viscott's "How to Live with Another Person" (Arbor House, 1974).

Am I recommending catering to public taste? I am recommending understanding and co-ordinating with public taste in order to exert influence upon it—an influence to increase the reading habit and sale of books, good books of all kinds.

I also recommend that the oral reviewer prepare a varied list of selections, at least three or four, of current outstanding books to submit to the program committees so that they can choose which they prefer. To offer only one title is a poor take-it-or-leave-it policy and only indicates your own limitations of one sort or another.

I offer, too, a word of warning. Beware of books that are privately printed, and this includes the so-called vanity or subsidy presses which generally operate without literary or editorial standards, royalty payments, promotion or distribution. Only a few exceptions can be made by the reviewer, notably in the case of poetry which seldom, unfortunately, has a better opportunity for getting into print. Even in this case, however, little can be done for a book that is not on the shelves of libraries or bookstores. If you are not certain or informed about the status of a publisher, consult a local bookstore manager or librarian.

I would advise that reviewers should not limit themselves to the hardcover book. A major trend in publishing has established the original release of new books of importance and much interest in paperback. An outstanding example was the monumental biographical novel "Sacajawea" by Anna Lee Waldo (see Chapter 10). Many others can be named, such as Gerald Green's "Holocaust," the John Jakes series and, of course, the books by Louis L'Amour. Accordingly, this field of production must have reviewers' attention.

chapter 6

Preparation of a Review

Your first step in preparing to review a book is to read it. If that seems to be an absurdly unnecessary statement, I assure you that it is not, for we see and hear countless examples of reviewers who have skimmed through and "hit the high spots" of a book. The trouble with this practice is that they completely miss the points of how and why those high spots evolved, and so have no way of knowing whether they are valid and meaningful or not. After all, the act of a minor character or the effect of a trivial circumstance can be all-important in shaping the climax in a novel, and not to get a fact right in non-fiction only shows that the reviewer was turning two or more pages instead of one at a time. A recent instance of this occurred in a New York paper's review of a biography whose subject was referred to by the reviewer as a Texan, when as a matter of fact the man had been born in Minnesota, had lived in Oklahoma and California, and had only invested in Texas oil property. The error was inexcusable and all the more so because the reviewer is a "name" who is supposed to be capable.

Of course, there are books which do not justify reading and should never have been published in the first place. If you find that to be so after some 50 pages, put the book down and use your eyesight and your time on another. Unlike the journalist reviewer, you can simply by-pass a poor book.

It is entirely true that some good books get off to a very slow and poor start (the editor has not done his job any better than the writer), but later pages more than repay the effort made in the beginning. Therefore, don't make a snap judgment in the first chapter. But, by and large, if you are still only plowing and not harvesting anything after three or four chapters, you can rather safely assume that the chances are nothing is going to grow here.

When you are reading, do so first as a *reader* and not as a reviewer. Just read. Then allow a period of time for digestion before beginning your professional approach. This enables you to get a more general reading reaction.

If you decide that this book is suitable for reviewing, then you are ready to settle down and begin writing your script or notes, referring to the book as needed for accuracy. Are you thinking, "If I am an oral reviewer, why write a review?" This script is basic for several reasons, and all of them good ones. First, a written script is necessary in order to get your thinking and the content of your review in shape and properly organized. It is also done so as to get facts, names, places, dates, sequence of events— in short, whatever detail you use—absolutely correct. Moreover, when you write your original ideas as generated by a book, you find that usually one thought opens the door to another.

But whether a complete script is written (as recommended for beginners) or notes or outline (which can suffice for the more experienced or professional), the extremely important matter of timing is set, as well as the pattern of organization of material.

This does not mean that you use every word which you have written when you finally present the review as a program. Not at all and heaven forbid, for then you would be guilty of the deadly act of "giving a paper." New wording and other phrasing will occur to you, for our English language is rich in synonyms. But the point of this whole matter is that a review prepared in script, notes, or outline will be organized and timed. You will not wander and drift and ramble. You will not forget major points and what you really wanted to say. You will not be a bore and commit the unforgivable sin of wasting time—both yours and the audience's.

Remember that, unlike the written review which can be returned to and be re-read, the oral review is heard then and there and that's it. You have only one chance with an audience for that particular program and book. Either you do your job or you don't; there is no going back to it for them or for you.

Written preparation in one form or another according to what is best for you is most essential because it protects you from the hazard of the strange tricks of your mind. From nervousness or for no good reason at all, the most experienced speakers suddenly find their minds completely blank. *You cannot trust your memory.*

All of use have had the experience of turning to introduce a dear friend and being unable to remember his name. A major point in your review can disappear from your mind just as easily. On social occasions this lapse of memory is merely embarrassing, but on the platform, at the microphone, or before a camera, it can ruin you.

Whatever you write that is original, you unconsciously and naturally memorize. If it's yours, you know it, no matter how the way you express it may vary. But even so, your confidence is increased by having notes. You are more relaxed and can give some of your attention to other matters of concern to a speaker besides the actual spoken words—matters to be discussed in the next chapter.

You will find that you use your notes less and less as time goes on. But even if you never look at them, have them. Don't think that it looks like a crutch or admission of lack of confidence. On the contrary, an audience can be greatly relieved to see that here is a speaker who has made some preparation.

If all that an audience can remember about you is that you had no notes, you have not given them very much. A well-trained parrot could have done as well. Of course notes should be in order, easily legible, and handled as inconspicuously as possible.

Extemporaneous speaking is definitely not for the beginner. It is a skill that requires much experience. By the time you have had sufficient experience for the poise, the sense of organization and timing and delivery technique necessary, as well as a sure sense of faultless grammar, you need no instruction. Besides, at this point we are not chiefly concerned with reviewing as an exhibit of public speaking mastery. Our accent here is on reviewing a book for the purposes we have named—how to prepare for it and how to present it. Our attention right now is on fundamentals. The book, not you, comes first.

Oscar Wilde once said that he "could resist anything but temptation." I charge you to resist it in the matter of using quotations. Limit the use of quotations from the author. Use them only for the effect of having the audience sample the quality of the book and not in order to reduce your own work through padding.

It is always important to indicate that you are quoting when you do use quotations. Remember that in reading one sees the signal of the quotation marks. An audience has no such guide; they must hear the quotation marks. Otherwise, those who have not yet read the book do not know what is yours and what is the author's. If that is a reviewer's purpose, it is completely illegitimate. When you quote, you borrow; you don't steal. It is a very simple matter to indicate what you are doing by the routine words, "quote" and "unquote," or by leading into quoted material with such phrases as "as the author says," "as (name of character) says," or "I want to share these words with you." This may seem clumsy, but soon it becomes a habit.

In an oral review you want to bring out the main points of value in the book—but not too many. The reason for this is again very simple and practical; when people are listening they can only remember so much and no more. If you give them too much, they become confused in their thinking and go away with a hodge-podge in their heads.

The main points of value, as you select and feature them within the book, become still more important when you interpret them in a way that relates and personalizes them to the present place and time. A point becomes a fact when it is brought home to one's own experience.

For example, when a character is a gossip, a hypochondriac, or a hypocrite, or any one of a dozen other unpleasant things, these are characteristics which we all know, come in contact with and have to deal with almost daily. Accordingly, whether the situation in the book is set in Copenhagen, London, Hong Kong, San Francisco, or New York, it might as well be in your own home town among people your audience knows. When you bring this out, you can see heads nod in instant recognition as they think of you-know-who. This reaction is basic in human nature. Most of us feel only what we know, and we know only what we experience.

Your interpretation of what is universal in a book will be most effective if you point out these similarities. Perhaps you perform your greatest service in doing this, not only for the book but also as a stimulus to people to think along parallel lines and to realize that it is foolish indeed to ask "for whom the bell tolls" when it tolls the same everywhere for everyone.

The very mention of that now well-known quotation which Hemingway took from the English poet John Donne leads to the suggestion that the reviewer should always explain and relate a title to an author's choice of it for the book's core of meaning. Usually, such a choice by the author or the editor applies to novels. Often it is a line or a phrase from a poem which is given within the book or on a front fly-leaf. When this is not done (as, for example, in "Gone with the Wind"), some research is necessary. After all, when a title is as striking and provocative as it should be, people wonder about it and like to know. In the case of Margaret Mitchell's novel, it meant something to readers to hear, perhaps for the first time, the Ernest Dowson poem "Cynara" which was the source of the title.

As previously mentioned, there should be a wordsketch of the author, brief and usually in the introductory part of your review. I do not agree with John Updike about even the written review when he admonishes in his book "Picked-Up Pieces" (Knopf, 1975), "Review the book not the [author's] reputation." The author and his reputation (if he is established and has produced before) should be measured against his latest book if for no reason other than sheer interest.

Another matter to be checked by the reviewer, and very carefully, is the correct pronunciation of names of persons and places referred to in a book. This also extends to the use of words and phrases in a foreign language. Don't think for one moment that you can "get by" without such checking in case you do not already know them. Most of our radio and TV announcers are horrible examples of this carelessness. There is always someone in your audience who *knows* what is right and that you are wrong. Nor will he or she hesitate to say so. After all, you are expected to know.

Where can you go to check on these matters? There are reference books in any library. There are the librarians themselves. There are teachers to consult in schools, colleges, and universities near you. There are always persons in almost any community now who travel widely, as well as those who are bilingual in background. In many cities there are consulates. There is always a way to find out what you do not know about words and names. Not knowing is no disgrace, but not making the effort to find out, is.

I doubt if any single thing is more important in preparing a review than keeping yourself keenly and constantly aware of the organization of your material, so that, when you present it, it will be built around one central idea. This will be the book's main idea which you stress. This will be the thought which your audience retains and which will attract and guide them in their own reading approach to the book.

A good book, lecture, or sermon contains a number of ideas, but one is always paramount. That is the one which you want to grasp and then to give to your audiences, remembering always that when we listen we are limited in what we can absorb. Therefore, there is a need for the oral reviewer to concentrate on a central idea so that the audience may do the same. Then they have something to take away with them. Would that more of the clergy realized this fact and organized their sermons accordingly. Then when a member of their congregation was asked, "What did he say today?", the member would not answer, "Oh, a lot of stuff. Gosh, I don't know."

By all means remain aware in reviewing that the simplest form of wording is the best. This is not your self-made opportunity to show off your vocabulary. On the contrary, it is mandatory for you to be clearly understood. Nothing is more desirable than a large and varied vocabulary which becomes enlarged and enriched every day of your life. But use it with judgment and taste for effect, not ostentation. This does not mean that you are to limit yourself to words of one syllable. But it does mean that you are not to use all the longest polysyllables in the dictionary. If you stop to think about it, the most potent words in our English language are simple: love, hate, fear, sex, life, war, death, God, art, book, young, old, home . . . This fact is not without significance and is one to be remembered.

The timing of a review varies, of course, according to the type of program. If you are on the air, the time is very definitely and exactly set. If you are presenting what is usually referred to as a full-length review from the platform, the time may range from 20 or 30 minutes (for certain men's luncheon groups) to 45 or 50 minutes.

Never speak for more than an hour, and preferably less.

The greatest compliment you can receive is to be told "It was just too short! I could listen to you for hours!" Nothing makes you feel better, but just don't believe it. Remember that you never hear those who repeat the refrain of the Christian martyrs, "How long, O Lord, how long?"

In public speaking of any kind, and as in all forms of art, one of the most important things to know is when to stop. Knowing when to put the last brush-stroke on a canvas, the last note on a music score, the last touch on a piece of sculpture, and when to say the final word, marks the artist.

Your review material should be flexible and elastic. The same book can be reviewed as well in 15 as in 50 minutes. The difference is a matter of condensation and expansion of detail both within its own content and your commentary. The shorter the time, the more difficult is your work and responsibility. Lord Chesterfield once expressed this fact best when he offered his apology for writing such a long letter because he did not have time to compose a short one.

Anyone can go on talking if he has the endurance, and if the audience has the same amount. But the professional sets a time limit and adheres to it. This calls for more and more careful, thoughtful selection of the material you plan to use, the points you must include and feature, the points you can and should leave out. Every word counts. Don't cling to the idea, as some writers and speakers do, that because Thomas Wolfe did not count them, neither should you.

Remember that the story of creation in Genesis is in only 400 words, and the Ten Commandments are given in 297 words. For Caesar there was the ultimate in brevity: "Veni, vidi, vici,-I came, I saw, I conquered." In this 20th century President Calvin Coolidge seems to have set the record for no waste of verbiage with his statement "I do not choose to run".

In this connection, there were some words spoken by Ernest Hemingway in an interview reported by *The Paris Review* which are memorable. He said in reference to his "Old Man and the Sea":

> It could have been over a thousand pages long [it was only a one hundred and forty] and had every character in the village in it and all the processes of how they were born and lived and were educated. That is done well by other writers. In writing you are limited by what has already been done well. And so I have tried to learn to do something else. I have tried to eliminate everything unnecessary to convey experience, so that after you read something it will become part of your experience and seem actually to have happened. This is hard to do and I have worked at it very hard.
>
> I had a good man and a good boy, and lately writers have forgotten that there still are such things. Then the ocean is worth writing about just as man is.
>
> I always try to write on the principle of the iceberg, seven-eighths of it under water for every part that shows.

I quote this "iceberg" principle not only as a point relative to the art of condensation but also as a point of proof of what a writer leaves unsaid for interpretation. As he continued in the same interview:

> It is hard enough to write books and stories without being asked to explain them. Also it deprives the explainers of work. Read for the pleasure of reading. Whatever else you find will be the measure of what you bring to it.

In concluding an oral review, I have found two methods which are most successful. *A summary of points* is very effective in the case of many non-fiction books, especially those of analysis and commentary on current events, history, and biography. Such a summary, sharpened by your final evaluation of the book's significance, leaves the audience with a neatly tied-together package.

In fiction and drama, however—and many times in biography and autobiography—a *provocative punch line of thought* is your best parting shot. This can be originial or, if especially apt, a quote which gives a strong final expression of the main idea, character, situation, or personality featured in the book and stressed by you in the review. Actually, this is in itself a form of summary, but one of essence, and therefore can be elaborated upon more subtly.

chapter 7

Delivery Technique

A review may be well prepared, but if it is poorly presented, little if anything is accomplished. And so we come now to the major characteristic of this form of reviewing. It is oral. This fact requires that a technique of oral delivery be fully as important as the content of the review. Indeed, the delivery is an integral part of the review, for the effectiveness and the success of an oral review depend in great part on the delivery.

As generations of men and women through the centuries have risen to speak or remained seated to listen, they have learned the truth of Aristotle's statement that "It is not enough to know what to say but how to say it" and also of the great Cicero's observation, "If truth were self-evident, oratory would be unnecessary." Unfortunately, truth is far from being obvious to the majority of the general public if, as, and when it appears in print. Therefore, with "oratory" necessary, what kind should it be? And more to the point, what kind of oratory should we have in oral book reviewing?

First of all, it must never show itself as deliberate oratory at all. It must be a sincere projection of thought and feeling through your voice, your manner, and your facial expressions. Above all, it must be *natural*. It must appear to be as natural for you to speak publicly as privately. This can require great effort on your part at first, but that effort must not be evident.

Practice at home is a good idea. But don't do it with your family. Usually a husband, parent, wife, sister or brother will give you either too much praise or too much criticism. Practice by yourself in front of a mirror and a clock. Watch yourself. Listen to yourself. What you say, the way you say it, how you look as you say it, are things you can judge without any fanfare, foolishness, or false modesty.

Nervousness? Of course, you will be nervous always, no matter how much experience is behind you. Whenever you reach a point of not being nervous in the opening moments of contact with an audience, you will be heading for trouble. That signals the difference between confidence and over-confidence. You can be quite confident and still be nervous, but when you are so over-confident as not to be in any way apprehensive, that is the time you are going to make a fool of yourself.

This initial nervousness diminishes and disappears altogether as you "get the feel" of an audience, as you establish contact with them. It's a great deal like plugging in an electrical connection. The same thing happens in social conversation with a stranger. You meet, and then you really get together and, as we say, "hit if off."

So, too, an audience becomes a composite personality. It can be friendly, warm, and responsive, or it can be reserved and cold. But the thing always to remember is that they are only people, just folks. This is something you must not only remember but also visualize in speaking before any radio microphone or TV camera, so that you remain aware of speaking to people and not just to an instrument.

Actually, the larger the audience the better for any speaker. One of the most trying incidents that I can recall was a review program which I was engaged to give one night at the home of a millionaire in a certain Texas city. Many such engagements are made for private dinner parties, but that one turned out to be entirely too private. The book requested by the hostess from my list was "Honourable Estate," Vera Brittain's powerful novel of women victimized by loveless marriages and without legal escape. However, when I arrived at the mansion I learned that my hostess was giving this program only for her husband. And so there sat my audience, just the two of them, in a room big enough for a hundred, but not big enough for the hatred it housed. There was nothing to do but figuratively close my eyes and imagine a normal audience situation.

The talented singer-actress-dancer Mary Martin put it this way in her memoir, "My Heart Belongs" (William Morrow, 1976), "I react to an audience. Give me four people and I'm on. Give me four hundred and I'm a hundred times more on . . . Live audiences give to performers; they contribute far more than they have any idea . . . One can feel them. Their very presence starts a kind of electricity, a chemistry which comes from the give-and-take of a performance."

It is impossible to stress sufficiently the need for naturalness as the outstanding quality in the delivery of a book review. You are not putting on an act. Even if you were, no course in dramatics, public speaking, or any allied subject could ever improve upon the complete set of instructions which you can read for yourself at the opening of Scene 2, Act 3 in *Hamlet*.

Speak the speech, I pray you, as I pronounced it to you, trippingly on the tongue: but if you mouth it, as many of your players do, I had as lief the town-crier spoke my lines. Nor do not saw the air too much with your hand, thus; but use all gently: for in the very torrent, tempest, and, as I may say, whirlwind of your passion, you must acquire and beget a temperance that may give it smoothness. O, it offends me to the soul to hear a robustious periwigpated fellow tear a passion to tatters, to very rags, to split the ears of the groundlings, who, for the most part, are capable of nothing but inexplicable dumbshows and noise: I would have such a fellow whipped for o'erdoing Termagant; it out-herods Herod: pray you, avoid it.

Be not too tame neither, but let your own discretion be your tutor: suit the action to the word, the word to the action; with this special observance, that you o'erstep not the modesty of nature: for anything so overdone is from the purpose of playing, whose end, both at the first and now, was and is, to hold, as 'twere, the mirror up to nature; to show virtue her own feature, scorn her own image, and the very age and body of the time his form and pressure. Now this overdone or come tardy off, though it make the unskilful laugh, cannot but make the judicious grieve; the censure of the which one must in your allowance o'erweigh a whole theatre of others. O, there be players that I have seen play, and heard others praise, and that highly, not to speak it profanely, that neither having the accent of Christians nor the gait of Christian, pagan, nor man, have so

strutted and bellowed, that I have thought some of nature's
journeymen had made men, and not made them well, they imitated
humanity so abominably.

Study these words, apply them, and you will have your
bachelor's, master's, and doctor's degrees in both dramatics and
public speaking. No one has ever added one jot or tittle to that
complete course by Will Shakespeare.

When you are called upon for your review program, it is
good practical psychology to have a copy of the book you are
reviewing with you. Placed on the lectern or table before you, the
book can be seen by the audience; their sensory reaction to its
jacket and physical appearance has an impression of value. It is
there before them, as well as you are; it shares the spot-light.

Your first act, of course, is the courtesy of responding to the
introduction which has been given you. This can be a simple
"Thank you, Mr., Mrs., or Miss Blank" or it can be a more fully
expressed appreciation of what has been said, with, perhaps, a
return compliment on that person's own reputation. But keep it
as brief as the introduction should have been.

It is highly important, when you take over the program, that
you come to your audience with a pleasant look on your face, not
a grim do-or-die one. After all, this should be the same look of
natural interest and greeting on your part as when you are
meeting an individual.

Do not begin speaking immediately. Allow time to get
yourself settled comfortably and for the audience to get settled
even more comfortably. Look at your watch and get the time in
mind.

During this initial pause of a few seconds, *have your eyes on your
audience*. We all like to be looked at, and this begins at once to
bring speaker and audience together. As you go on, except for
glances at your notes, keep your eyes on the audience. This
maintains the personal connection between you and your listeners.

Always, your *first objective is to be heard*. This is basic.
Therefore, in any room or auditorium of any size, and with any
audience beyond a very small group, the most sensible and

companionable thing you can do is to ask at the beginning, "Can you hear me?" At once you will see the heads of those on the back rows nod or shake and hear several vocal negatives or affirmatives. Even the presence of a public address system microphone does not eliminate this recommendation. As a matter of fact, a poor microphone or one set for too much volume and too close to you can cause its own particular brand of trouble. In that case, just turn it off or away from you.

Speak slowly. This does not mean a draggy largo—it does mean setting a pace which allows each word to be heard. Naturally, you will vary this tempo for effect and apropos to what you are saying. In this way, monotony is avoided just as it is in using your different levels of voice.

Timing for the effect of a pause in order to allow a thought or a question to penetrate and "sink in" is a valuable part of delivery technique. An outstanding master of this was the great comedian Jack Benny. He did it for laughs. You do it for thought. The ends differ, but the process is one and the same.

Another point to remember is that it can be helpful to your audience, especially on radio, if you take a second to spell out the author's name in cases where the name is foreign or strange to them. After all, if a person goes into a library or a bookshop to get the book, forgets the title, and says that the author's name "sounded something like (a vague sort of grunt)," the bookseller or the librarian is stymied.

Whenever one stands before an audience, a well-groomed appearance is important. For a man this involves, as usual, less than it does for a woman. But in both cases there is the need to look your best according to what is suitable for the time and place. It should be obvious that a morning or a luncheon program rules out a tuxedo or a cocktail or dinner dress. On the other hand, unless the group and affair are most informal, an afternoon tea or evening program definitely calls for a more formal accent on dress.

Do not, however, let this be a signal to show off everything in your wardrobe, plus all the family jewels. You are to adorn a platform, but what you wear is not to distract attention from what you are there to say. This is a book review program, not a style show. The audience is there to remember the book and not your dress.

Begin the program in the clothes which you are going to keep on. Don't appear gloved and mink-stoled and then gradually emerge from this splendor as if going into a strip-tease, removing one accessory after another. The audience's attention is glued then to what you are doing and not at all to what you are saying. In such cases, the author, the publisher, and the bookseller—all should appear with shotguns.

A woman will find it wise to select the color of her dress carefully. One never knows the color of the background curtain before which one will be standing, and only rarely the color of the shoulder bouquet of flowers to be given her to wear. A pink dress topped with red carnations can be a rather horrible sight, especially in front of a chartreuse curtain.

A word of warning also to the man who stands twirling a watch chain or a key ring, fingering and jingling the coins in his pocket, or putting on and taking off his eyeglasses over and over again.

In all these instances, heaven help the book which is supposed to be reviewed.

In addition, a program is not the time for taking one's exercise. Don't stroll up and down the platform: stand still and wait to take your walk later.

To continue these practical specifics, it is most unwise to eat a full meal just before a program. If you must participate in a luncheon or a dinner immediately prior to your program, eat very sparingly. Otherwise you will find yourself speaking and combatting nervous indigestion at the same time. The result can be not only a poor review but even a heart attack. When one considers the soppy creamed chicken, the tired old filets, the green pea marbles, and the soggy baked potatoes which all too often comprise the routine menu, no real martyrdom is suffered by waiting until after the program to relax and enjoy what you want.

Try also to avoid the fatigue of a reception line before a program. Suggest that your part of that is better done after the program, when people have questions to ask and points to discuss with you. In this way, all your energy is conserved for the work you are here to do which is reviewing a book and giving a good program. After you talk, you can afford the exhausting ordeal of personally greeting and talking with every member of a large audience, but not before.

There is yet another matter of importance in the platform manner, a matter of behavior even more undesirable in public than in private. Stated as simply as possible, it is not to show temperament. Many things occur during a program. People cough and sneeze and cannot help it. Somebody gets sick and has to leave. Somebody else suddenly has to seek the lounge. Another remembers that she forgot to turn off the gas under the roast at home, or that it's car pool time to pick up several members of the next generation who have never heard of walking. There are always some who come in late because of the parking problem. At times a dog or a cat wanders in. A woman drops her pocketbook and a compact or a lipstick or a fifty-cent piece rolls for seemingly several miles. Mrs. Jones finds herself sitting in a draft. Mrs. Smith is too hot.

These and many other disturbances happen—all the little personal emergencies which nobody can help. Of course they bother you, but you must ignore them. Nothing is more ill-mannered in a speaker than to stop and draw attention to a person who cannot help being a momentary disturbance. It is embarrassing and humiliating to the person and only shows the speaker's lack of poise.

I remember a time when a well-known poet came to lecture at the University of Chicago while I was a freshman there. It was a long and eagerly awaited event and old Mandel Hall had a capacity audience that cold winter night. The poet came on stage and began reading from her latest collection of poems. But suddenly a radiator began making the noise which only a radiator can make under a condition of extreme internal torture. Of course somebody went for the janitor to get the nuisance under control, but it was not so easy to get the speaker under control. She left the stage in an exhibit of temperament which I regret is all that any of us can remember of her performance that night.

On the other hand, I recall a lecture by another speaker in

the course of which he noticed a woman trying to close a window by her seat and unable to pull it down. Without any break in his lecture, and without creating any situation, he walked over and closed the window, smiled, and returned to the podium. The incident was memorable for perfect poise.

This is not always easy, as I know from my own experience. During a review of a biography of Cleopatra a number of years ago in Texarkana, a cyclone struck. All the lights in the municipal auditorium went out just as we had Cleopatra on the Nile with Marc Anthony. It was a scenic effect a bit too dramatic and my knees were the consistency of gelatin, but, in order to avert a panic, there was nothing to do but to go on talking until the lights came on again.

In short, anything can happen during a program, and sooner or later it does. Just keep the program going.

After concluding your review, do not break that final thought which you are leaving with the audience and "disconnect" yourself from them too abruptly by walking off on the last word. Do as you did at the beginning and stand still a few seconds, your eyes still with your audience. This parting pause serves as a sort of period, a sign-off instead of a break-off. It allows time to readjust, both for them and for you.

Unless you have considerable platform experience and a good knowledge of literature, I do not recommend that you ask for questions from the audience after a review program. With small group or club audiences, perhaps yes, but not with public audiences. Such question-and-answer periods can be interesting, of course, but they can also lead to trouble if a crackpot is present and looking for an argument. If, however, you do ask for questions and you receive one which you cannot answer, say so. Don't gamble a guess unless you admit that it's a guess.

chapter 8

Interviewing

Almost inevitably, it seems, when a reviewer is on radio or television, the authors who go on tour to promote their books present themselves for interview. Usually this is arranged by their publishers or agents. Accordingly, a few words about this can come in handy to the reviewer.

Interviewing is all too often handled as just a routine matter. Ask a few questions more pert than pertinent, get a few answers, and that's it. Anybody can do it on any newspaper, magazine, radio, or TV staff. This is *not* so.

Interviewing presupposes that there is knowledge about the person to be interviewed and about his or her work. In the case of authors, the very first requisite is that their books have been read by the interviewer. Nothing is more horrendous to writers than to be asked a lot of silly questions by a person completely ignorant of their books. To avoid this all too common situation, a list of suggested questions is sometimes supplied by the publisher. This sort of manufactured, pre-packaged interview is a makeshift thing and lacks the spontaneity most desirable, but at least it saves many authors from the inanities of reporters and commentators who never read the books nor even see them.

Interviewing can be fun and an exciting and stimulating exchange, or it can be dull and draggy. Men and women who are excellent writers are not always articulate as speakers socially, and an interview is a form of social intercourse, hopefully. Why? Because there are two persons who are talking, and if this is done *naturally* then the interview will be a success.

Here, too, as in the presentation of a book review, the quality of naturalness in your manner is so very attractive to your audience. Firing questions like a machine is not good interviewing. The questions and answers should combine into a conversation about the author and the book, but with the interviewer directing it so that the author does most of the talking.

Jot down in advance a few questions that the book has raised in your own mind about its message or characters or situations; before you begin the interview, ask your guest if he or she likes these potentials for discussion or if there are other points he or she would prefer. This is a gesture of sheer courtesy.

If research has been involved in writing the book, be sure to ask about that in the interview. Authors love to tell how hard they have worked, and the public is interested and impressed. Usually, too, there are good anecdotes in all research work.

Never fail to bring in personal touches, such as the author's background, and how and why this book came to be written.

By all means have the book with you and announce and refer to its title often. If you are on camera, hold it up so that it can be clearly seen. After all, the purpose of the interview is not just entertainment, but promotion of the book.

If the author is addicted to monologues, keep your control of the interview (and time) by interrupting in such a way as to re-direct a question to get more specific or to come to some graceful conclusion.

Authors like to be asked about their future work, even when they act cagey about it. I recall interviewing Joshua Logan about his 1976 book of memoirs, and he woefully told me that on a previous program someone kept referring to him in the past tense as if he were through with writing, producing, directing—dead and buried.

I have interviewed a sizable majority of today's outstanding authors and I soon learned, and hope now to assure you, that there is no reason to be nervous about it. The bigger they are, the friendlier and humbler they are—always grateful for help in promoting their books. Only the pip-squeak who is riding the crest of a momentary celebrity cult or who heads a stable of "ghosts" who do his writing for him will take a superior attitude to cover his vulnerability. In such cases (and they are minimal) just reduce the time and let him hang himself on the noose of his own foolishness, which will be as apparent to the audience as it is to you.

Never interview an author whose work you cannot honestly recommend. Don't cheapen *your* work. You have set certain standards professionally. Maintain them.

chapter 9

Your Public, Your Market, Your Tools

The potential of work for the oral reviewer is enormous and steadily increasing wherever popular educational entertainment is in demand.

Not only clubs of every kind and school and church auxiliary organizations, but also convention groups and many business firms want these programs. Department stores and banks, for example, have found that nothing serves the promotional purpose of public relations in attracting large audiences better than this means of giving the people what they want and enjoy. The fact that such programs draw the higher literate level of the public tends to add prestige to the company. Small-town radio and TV stations which are free of too much network commitment can well use the review program both as a public service feature and for sale to local sponsors.

But again for the practical approach—how and where should beginners launch their careers in this profession? The best place to start is right in your own backyard. Just let a local church group or club know that you are available, for free, and nature will take its course. Nature will continue on its course after your program. If the audience liked it, the all-important word-of-mouth advertising begins and you will soon have all the work you can handle. If they did not like it, the same principle operates in reverse.

But you take no chances either way if you attend to your publicity as you should. After all, publicity is your only remuneration at first, and you are entitled to insist upon it. The way to take care of this matter is to ask the program committee chairman if a publicity notice has been sent to the local newspaper or newscaster. If not, mail this in yourself, including your name and the title of the book to be reviewed, of course. Usually this goes to the women's news editor of the paper, but you can check on this matter. Always keep such press clippings, preferably several extra copies, for you will have need for these later to send to the publisher's publicity department.

There is no hard and fast rule to put down concerning when you should stop your non-professional career and put it on a professional basis of fee. All that can govern this is the amount of experience which makes you ready to be worth a charge. In most cases, where a reviewer has been doing an appreciable amount of work (at least a program or two a month on a variety of books for different audiences), a little over a year could serve as adequate apprenticeship. If one does less work and therefore has acquired less experience, then at least another year should be allowed.

When, however, you do announce to the program chairmen who call upon you that you have set a professional policy, do not deviate from it. Your only exceptions should be for out-and-out charity organizations which you wish to favor accordingly.

Nothing is more unbusiness-like and nothing will boomerang against you professionally more than to cut fees for certain groups. Despite the fact that the ladies swear to keep the matter as secret as their weight and age, it will leak out. Then you are confronted by others who very rightly want to know why you charged them more than you did so-and-so. Finding a satisfactory answer to that question would be much more difficult than finding good books to review. By all means pass up the opportunity for a program engagement rather than become involved in such a situation. Leave the special sale prices and mark-downs to the supermarkets. Oral book reviewing is a profession.

As in any other profession, the matter of fees is set by the individual relative to the local conditions and degree of popular demand for that individual's time and work. In order to offer some scale or range to go by, it can be suggested that a minimum could begin at fifty dollars and then develop to seventy-five, a hundred, and up. When travel is involved, a fee plus expenses is a recommended way to operate.

If that travel ever has to include a trip such as I had once on a freight train with one car for passengers to share with a two-week-old calf crying for its mother every mile of the way, then I suggest a slight addition to the expense account for something to steady the nerves.

Obviously, the matter of program fee is one which has to be decided according to the best of one's personal judgment. Ours is a profession in which you will never reach a bracket level of income that can cause you and the Internal Revenue Department any severe headaches. But it is one which can provide a good living. How good depends on your ability, your location, and your definition of "good living" in the best sense of the words.

A reviewer cannot expect publishers to supply review copies of books until and unless the reviewer becomes professionally established and has publicity to prove it. This further explains my recommendation in the preceding chapter that press notices of programs be sent to the publisher of the book reviewed. These clippings give the publisher something to refer to when he receives your inquiry for review copies of other books on his list. These lists or catalogues are freely supplied on request and are usually put out twice a year.

In the beginning, the best thing to do is to develop close contact with a local bookshop, so that the owner or manager knows you and your work, for very often dealers have advance copies of books and will cooperate with you. Otherwise, you use the library or buy your books.

The "tools of the trade" are many, and a reviewer needs and should use them all. First and foremost among these necessary reference books is the dictionary. Do not assume that you can check this off because you already have one. It is probably as old as you are and in no way up to date with the hundreds of new words added to our language in recent years. A new dictionary is essential at least every ten years. There are several excellent college edition dictionaries on the market: "Webster's New

World," "American Heritage," "Random House," and the "Harper Dictionary of Contemporary Usage" as a supplement. Naturally, nothing is more valuable and useful than the unabridged dictionary, and this is recommended as a very definite addition to your library.

Next on the list is an encyclopedia. If you have the space for a multi-volume set, nothing is more desirable. But if space is a problem, then the single volume of the Columbia, for instance, will serve you well.

Highly important, too, is a good modern biographical dictionary. The same is true of a thesaurus. But most frequently overlooked is the need for a new atlas. With our world no longer what it used to be in its man-made divisions and names, we all need to locate the geography of current literature. The reviewers need to know this and then to pass on such information to their audiences. To read that a man or woman was born in a town we never heard of means nothing to us, but when we learn that it was near a place which we do know, it literally makes all the difference in the world to us. Perhaps even personal memories or some cross-reference in reading experience may be evoked.

A good anthology of poetry and one of quotations, as well as the complete Bible (Old and New Testaments) and a complete Shakespeare are also of great help in reviewing. Such are the basic tools for ready reference. Only the readiness in you to use them completes the workshop.

In fact, this brings us to the final and over-all need of the book reviewer, which is to continue actively, vigorously, endlessly his or her own education. There are many ways and opportunities to do this, and all of them are good. The reading which is implicit in the very nature of the work of reviewing books is in itself contributory to this education. But this is not enough.

In or near your town, wherever you live today, there is a college or a university with an extension department which offers courses of study. There is also a public library with a trained librarian to locate books on any subject for you.

What are the courses and the subjects which can contribute most to you and your work as a reviewer? First of all, the study of English and American literature is your special province, but not only the literature itself. The history of literature is the survey needed to give you proper perspective. History in general is obviously a source of endless potential for understanding the very foundation of literature. But the history of what man has done is extended, deepened, highlighted by the study of Comparative Religions, Philosophy, and Anthropology for all that they reveal of how and what man has believed and thought in developing his life and the culture he has evolved. This not only forms the imprint of civilization but also gives an understanding approach to the Arts of our heritage and our creation.

For the person who has had little or no previous study in any of these subjects, general introductory survey courses would be best to begin with. But if one is working on his own, there are any number of books which serve the purpose very well, such as Will and Ariel Durant's "Story of Civilization" (Simon and Schuster series, eleven volumes to date).

Highly recommended, too, is the study of at least one other language, especially for the dimension it adds to self-expression and for the benefit of reading its literature in all its original beauty. Which language—let it be of your choice. Personally, I know of none richer in literary treasure than French. But Spanish, Italian, or German may be preferable to you for personal or regional reasons.

This constant expansion of adult education for us should not be limited to academic study. Just as much value is to be gained from travel, from attending the theater, from hearing all the great music that you can, and from going to art exhibitions whenever these are available and possible. Today such opportunities are available and possible for more people than ever before.

We flick a switch and hear fine music. We get in our cars and tour, and wherever we go there is history to learn and the works of man and Nature to be seen. It is all there just for the looking and the learning. This is our culture: what is around us and behind us, plus our cultivation of these things and of ourselves.

All such experience can enrich and stimulate us so as to increase our understanding of all that we read in books. We catch nuances of meaning as well as metaphors and references which otherwise would escape us. We acquire new material and resources to use in our own way. We add not only to our knowledge and information but also to our emotional and spiritual equipment. We are better prepared to meet the minds which open to us upon the printed pages of the books, new and old, which we review. We are better able to relay this meeting of minds to our audiences, so that books are introduced and interpreted to readers in a way which both heightens and deepens their reading interest.

We have one serious handicap. Unfortunately, the opportunity of hearing good English spoken well is all too infrequent today. A few national newscaster analysts afford this opportunity; still fewer announcers, sometimes the clergy and those in the upper level of politics contribute to the rare sound of our language at its best in daily life.

Fortunately, however, recordings are now available at stores and libraries, so that you can hear the spoken word of masters such as Winston Churchill, Franklin Roosevelt, Laurence Olivier, and a number of English and American writers who read expertly and effectively.

With the public, especially children, exposed contantly to the murder of grammar and diction by TV gunmen and gangsters, it has become more and more important for all of us who work with the spoken word to do so with full awareness of our responsibility to use and present both the power and the beauty of our language. We are woefully outnumbered, but at least we man a mighty fortress.

There is reason to add a note of warning. Any young profession inevitably encounters a certain amount of jealousy and its attendant manifestations among certain types in an older profession. This can and rather absurdly does occur in the attitude of some journalist reviewers toward oral reviewers. It is nothing which time and good work do not efface. Both forms of book reviewing are needed and are here to stay. If reviewers in both fields are attending to their work and are fully alert to its purpose in serving the reading public, there will be, as there should be, only the complete cooperation and mutual respect of colleagues in a single endeavor for one cause and one only— books.

chapter 10

An Offer of First Aid

In this last chapter you will find a selection of sample scripts of my book reviews of different lengths for different media and purposes. Naturally, I mave confined these selections to books which are standard and give promise of remaining in print and available for you. This factor of necessity ruled out much of the contemporary, of course. I have also been guided to select an assortment of various types of books such as the novel, novelette, drama, humor, biography, etc. The timing ranges from a 10- and 14-minute radio segment (allowing for opening and closing announcements) to a 55-minute book review lecture presentation. Different treatments from a timing standpoint can be seen in the full-length review of "The Nazarene" and then the very condensed version; this demonstrates the flexibility necessary in handling the same material for different situations.

You will notice that in all these scripts the regular rules of punctuation are not generally followed. This is deliberate, because these scripts have been written for oral delivery, not reading. An oral reviewer develops his or her own system of personal signals, just as in one's notes or outline. I have also deliberately left the dating of these reviews intact relative to when they were presented.

Making such a limited choice from hundreds of reviews was quite an experience in itself, as the total collection really amounted to a survey of several decades of twentieth-century literature. That's not very long in the perspective of any literary history, but long enough to show the vigor, variety, vitality of literary production before, during and after two world wars, plus other social upheavals.

The books were good, and many now out of print need reissue or reprint for today's and tomorrow's generations. In fact, I based a recent course at Southern Methodist University on re-discovery of books such as Romain Rolland's "Jean Christophe," George Santayana's "The Last Puritan," Hervey Allen's "Anthony Adverse," Ayn Rand's "The Fountainhead," Tom Lea's "King Ranch," Marcia Davenport's "Of Lena Geyer," Somerset Maugham's "The Razor's Edge," Nevil Shute's "On the Beach," William Humphrey's "Home from the Hill," Edgar Lee Masters' "Spoon River Anthology," Margaret Armstrong's "Fanny Kemble," Louis Bromfield's "The Rains Came," Daphne du Maurier's "Rebecca," Edna Ferber's "A Peculiar Treasure," Marjorie Rawlings' "The Yearling," John Marquand's "The Late George Apley," A.J. Cronin's "The Citadel," James Hilton's "Lost Horizon," Pearl Buck's "The Good Earth," Axel Munthe's "The Story of San Michele," Rachel Carson's "Silent Spring," Anne Frank's Diary, short stories by Mark Twain, Dorothy Parker, Eudora Welty, Katherine Anne Porter, plus the books reviewed on the following pages.

It is not enough to have a modern reading background limited to Sinclair Lewis, F. Scott Fitzgerald, Willa Cather, John Steinbeck, Theodore Dreiser, William Faulkner, Ernest Hemingway, nor a handful of cultists. Professional book reviewers have little time for nostalgia. It's the new book just off the press that must reach the public; this is our primary concern. Most especially this is desirable for the new author who needs all the help possible.

Gone with the Wind

By Margaret Mitchell

July 1936

For the first time in a long, long while here is an honest-to-goodness *novel* in the good old-fashioned sense of telling a story for the sake of the story as it evolves from human character,—and not as a contribution to psychology, philosophy, history, religion, sociology, or any such academic purpose. And this story is told for 1040 pages with never a let-down in interest—unlike "Anthony Adverse," which, you recall, after its first 200 pages or so was never quite the same sweet Anthony.

Margaret Mitchell's achievement is remarkable in many ways. Most remarkable is the fact that it is her first novel. Born and reared in Atlanta—sprung from a family who have lived in and fought for Georgia ever since the Revolutionary War—feature writer on the *Atlanta Journal*—she has been working on this novel for 7 years. Never were 7 years better spent, for she has not turned out just another story of the South, but, in my opinion she has written *the* story of the South—the finest novel that has yet come from below the Mason-Dixon line. The chief reason for this is that the line does not mark the boundary of her book—nor her brain.

The trouble with most Southern writers has been that they have started out to tell a story and ended up by fighting the Civil War all over again and trying to start another one. They have all written histories, legends, rhapsodies, or propaganda. Miss Mitchell is too much of a narrative artist for this. She has not lost herself in the mists of sentiment nor in the fog of prejudice. She writes objectively, realizing that she's telling a story which, like

61

all stories, has two sides. Her pen is not dripping in sorghum, but is dipped in ink—and the result is a book, not a buckwheat cake.

History is her background and there she keeps it—as the background to and for her characters. History is told through their lives—they live it—just as we are living ours. They are not just names, puppets, characters in a book—but people whom you'll live and love and laugh and hate and grow old with and know better than any in the flesh about you. It is the best kind of historical novel—the kind that *is* a novel, aware of the fact. Events are of human interest only as they affect human beings.

And what people they are—these people who are gone with the wind—the hot wind and then the chill wind that swept over them 75 years ago. Sang Omar centuries before, "We come like water and like wind we go." But wind—strong winds leave marks —marks of destruction—and what has been destroyed must be rebuilt—and all this takes—makes strong people—and such a person was and is Scarlett O'Hara, Miss Mitchell's Becky Sharp.

When we first meet her only a gentle breeze is blowing—the light spring breeze of April in northern Georgia, rippling the peach and dogwood blossoms, carrying the hum of darkies' voices in from the fields as the sun sinks to rest behind the endless acres of rich red clay earth plowed and waiting for its cotton seeds on the beautiful O'Hara plantation. And the year, of course, is 1861.

Scarlett is 16—and disturbingly beautiful. The adverb is significant, for hers is a beauty that you just don't look at and admire—it does things to you. And it was doing things to Stuart and Brent Tarleton sitting beside her in the cool shade of the Colonial veranda—Scarlett in her twelve yards of flowered muslin billowing over hoops calling attention to the incredible perfection of a 17-inch waist, the smallest in three counties—the tightly fitting basque displaying just the tantalizing outline of her breast. In every outward respect a most lady-like young lady—except for her eyes. Scarlett's eyes were not lady-like. They were female. And they were reason enough why the handsome Tarleton twins were not at all downcast at having just been returned from the University of Georgia, the fourth university to expel them in two years—the Tarleton twins, 19 years old and each 6 feet 2 inches of solid virility with every qualification of the dashing Southern

gentleman—they could raise good cotton—ride like the devil—
shoot straight—dance divinely—carry their liquor like a flower—
and put Romeo in the shade of a magnolia tree. Their family had
more money—more horses—more slaves—than anyone in the
county. Why bother with education? That was all right for the
poor Crackers—who needed it—having nothing else.

The boys were excited—there's going to be a war. Scarlett is
excited—there's going to be a barbecue.

Day before yesterday General Beauregard showed those
Yankees the Confederacy meant business when he fired them out
of Fort Sumter—but this bores Scarlett, as it was the fashion for
any serious talk to bore young ladies—young ladies were meant
to be amused, adored,—not talked to about things they couldn't
and shouldn't understand—things like States' Rights and
Secession and Abolition and Abe Lincoln and War and Politics
and Business—not being interested in things of vital concern was
being feminine and charming, and the boys beamed upon her.
How many dances will she give them tomorrow at the ball after
the barbecue at the Wilkes plantation? She has none left. But
maybe she would manage to save them one if they tell her a
secret? Very well, then—there's an engagement to be announced
at the Wilkes party!—Ashley Wilkes' to his cousin, Melanie
Hamilton of Atlanta! Much to their surprise Scarlett goes quite
white at this—promises them all the waltzes—and lets them call
for their horses, mount, and gallop off without ever suggesting
that they stay for dinner.

Scarlett needed time out. She was upset. Badly. In fact, her
heart was breaking—a very painful sensation just at the twilight
hour. This simply could *not* be true about Ashley's engagement—
it just couldn't be. Why, Ashley had been taking her out at least
once a week ever since he'd been back from his Grand Tour of
Europe—she was in love with him—he was in love with her—
true, he had never said so, but she knew he was—and was just
waiting to propose . . . and now what on earth could have
happened? For the first time in her life Scarlett was not getting
what she wanted—and there was nothing on earth she wanted as
much as Ashley Wilkes—Ashley, so blond, so mysteriously,
fascinatingly different from every other man she had ever known.

Ashley who could ride and shoot better than all the other men and yet cared so little about it—caring so much more for things she and none of the rest of them cared or knew about at all— things like books and music and theatre and pictures and ideas— Ashley so somehow removed and remote from everyone around him even while taking a leading part in everything they did— Ashley so always out of reach—Ashley becoming engaged to his little plainfaced colorless cousin, Melanie, when he really wanted Scarlett. Scarlett took what she wanted. So did everyone else she knew. Why didn't Ashley?

The answer—so beyond her—was that, unlike her own simple elemental nature, Ashley's was complex. All the Wilkes were. That's why they were wont to marry their cousins—finding understanding only in their own family. They were so different from the other planters around Atlanta. They were the old aristocrats from Savannah and Charleston with generations of refinement and education behind them; they spoke another language. The Atlanta section was new—the people nouveau riche—men like Gerald O'Hara, Scarlett's father, go-getters, the first generation of the landed gentry, working and buying their way into the Southern planters' heritage and society—and marry- ing its daughters.

This combination can be seen in no more interesting exam- ple than in Scarlett herself—Scarlett who had inherited all of her father's rough force—ruthless determination—indomitable will —and only the veneer of her mother's gentility. Scarlett, who wanted so terribly to be a gentlewoman, a great lady like her mother—and simply couldn't be because she wasn't—inside. Desperately her Mammy and Mrs. O'Hara had worked with her, taming, polishing, teaching—and Scarlett had acquired the polish and learned the lessons—and remained Scarlett—Gerald O'Hara's daughter.

Scarlett worshiped her mother and all that she stood for— but it cramped her style. Scarlett was late Renaissance—or twentieth century—anything but 1861 old South. If in Boston the Cabots spoke only to the Lodges and the Lodges only to God, in the South they did not even take such chances. Southern society was as tightly laced as its women's waists—which is saying a good deal if you could have seen Scarlett holding her breath and holding on to the bedstead while her Mammy pulled her in. It was a society bound by the most rigid code of etiquette and artificial behavior imaginable. It wasn't so much a life as an art —a highly romantic art in a classic form. Reality was a thing never to be faced—without an apology and a blush. Knighthood was in flower and a beautiful flower it was—the most decorative ever to adorn the pages of American history—but it was a flower, and the fate of flowers is to be pressed between the pages of history. The tempo was adagio—a Mozart symphony. And Scarlett was made for the jazz beat.

Sit back now like a well-mannered little nit-wit and let Ashley go? Indeed not! Scarlett was the sort of woman constitutionally unable to allow any other woman to be admired and desired more than she. She looked upon all women only in the light of competitors. She cared nothing about women—they existed only for the exquisite pleasure and purpose of being vanquished by herself. Just let her see a man pay one bit of attention to any other woman—and Scarlett, even though she cared nothing about him, was after him. And she never failed. In the first place, nature was on her side. She was so gorgeous—and she knew every trick from Eve down the line. She didn't like these tricks—she considered them as silly as they were—she didn't like the clinging vine, downcast eyes, fluttering eyelids, demurely infantile "Oh, you great big wonderful man," swooning technique of the day—she couldn't swoon if she wanted to, healthy little animal that she was,—and she had more sense than any man she ever knew—but if she had to appear senseless and swoon to get them—get them she could and would and did. She had taken away every girl's beau in northern Georgia—and now Ashley, the one she loved, was being taken from her.

Carefully, deliberately with the coldly calculating intelligence of a general planning a campaign, Scarlett laid her plans for tomorrow.She would wear her best dress—the one with the lowest neckline—she would flirt with every man at the party —get them all around her—be the belle of the ball—arouse Ashley's jealousy and make him regret his mistake—and if that didn't work, she would play her trump card—she'd just tell him that she loved him—and then, well, then being a gentleman he'd just have to marry her. Ashley was shy—didn't think he had a chance—why hadn't she thought of this before? It was so simple. And so, as Scarlett knelt with her family while her mother read the evening prayers to them and to their darkies after dinner, she decided to wear her green plaid taffeta with the flounces and green velvet ribbons that made her eyes look like emeralds. Thus was a barbecue to become a slaughter.

And so, all unaware of the fact that human destiny has a way of eluding even twelve yards of green taffeta, Scarlett prepared herself the next morning while Mammy, who knew her well enough to be suspicious, lectured her on how to behave—made her eat a breakfast the size of a dinner so that she would have no appetite for the barbecue even if her stays had permitted it, because it was the mark of a lady only to nibble most delicately when she was out, as if the thought and consumption of food were matters much too gross for her—otherwise it might look as if there wasn't enough to eat at home. And then came the succession of petticoats—finally the green taffeta above which Scarlett's shoulders rose like two crests of white foam—and so into the carriage with her sisters—and off to the Wilkes'.

The description of that gala scene—the resurrection of its atmosphere with all its old-world charm is a word-picture you will treasure—the dainty elegance of the ladies—the soft-spoken gallantries of the men—the subdued festive glee of the negroes scurrying about waiting on them—the clink of tall frosted glasses —the pungent smoke of the barbecue in the air—the lazy spring breeze already heavy with heat—it *was* a picture—misty and dreamy like a Corot or Watteau—a picture of plenty—of peace— of ease and enjoyment of ease—of undisturbed order and tranquility—of security—of dignity and tradition—of well-mannered, carefree gaiety. These were a people apart—these ladies and gentlemen at play in this lovely picture,—surely nothing could touch them—hurt—happen to them? And yet, what was the tension to be sensed beneath the smooth surface—that drew the men together in little groups to talk and frown, their eyes flashing with exictement. . . .

But now those groups are broken up—Scarlett O'Hara has arrived and her presence is felt like a flame. She is at her radiant best and every other light is dimmed as she gives each man a look and word that makes him feel he is the one and only. The queen holds court and the other women become just so many ladies-in-waiting—quite literally waiting. Only two men are exceptions. One is Ashley Wilkes. Every time she looks up she sees him—not looking and coming to her, but staying and going right on talking to Melanie Hamilton. What in the world can two people find so much to be talking about? She catches the sound of Melanie's sweet shy voice: "But I fear Mr. Thackeray is not as much of a gentleman as Mr. Dickens" . . . What rot to be talking about—about men one didn't even know.

The other man conspicuous by his absence at her side is a stranger—a visitor—the tallest, darkest, handsomest one Scarlett has ever seen in her life. Every time she steals a look at him she finds him looking at her—looking at her as no man ever has—his eyes laughing—can he possibly be laughing at her? A look so knowing and frankly appraising, without any of the polite deference and respect to which she is accustomed, that her feelings are divided between the pleasantly exciting thrill of attracting such attention and the uncomfortable realization that too much of her bosom is showing. "Why is he looking at me like that—like he knows all about me—like he's seeing me without my shimmy?" For the first time Scarlett is in the presence of someone capable of disturbing her as much as she disturbs others. She knows she should resent such a look and she does—and yet—she looks again . . . Who is he? Rhett Butler—the famous and infamous Rhett Butler of Charleston—disinherited son of one of the South's oldest and finest families—expelled from West Point —traveled all over the world—terribly brilliant—terribly successful—terribly wicked—terribly fascinating. Why had he been disinherited? For taking a young lady out buggy-riding in Charleston and having an accident and not getting her back until almost morning—and then not even proposing—and when the young lady's brother challenged him to a duel next day, Rhett, instead of letting himself be killed like a gentleman, killed the brother—imagine—Scarlett imagined and stole another look. He caught her eye and actually—winked . . . The truth of the matter was that in Rhett Butler, Scarlett has met her male counterpart —not only her equal, but her superior—her Waterloo. That's uncomfortable enough—and with Ashley paying absolutely no attention to her—what do all these other men around her matter? How could she get Ashley alone? Her chance came that afternoon in the library—and Scarlett made the most of it. She told him that she loved him—that she knew he loved her, not Melanie. Why did Ashley suddenly look so white, so miserable? Her heart ached for him as he took her hand as he would a child's and told her she must forget what she had said—as he would try to forget —that they were different, too different ever to be happy together. His voice went on gently, tenderly reasoning, but the reasoning was lost on Scarlett as her true self blazed forth in rage—the rage of a woman rejected. Forgetting completely that she was sup-posed to be a young lady, she cursed like a trooper, and as Ashley closed the door behind him, she picked up a very substantial vase and smashed it to smithereens.

"Now that," said a voice from behind the sofa, "is too much",—and Rhett Butler stood up. He had been stretched out there trying to take a nap when they had come in and he couldn't very well make his presence known during such a scene. He had heard every word—he, of all people, to witness her humiliation,— and now his eyes were laughing at her more than ever . . .

Somehow or other, Scarlett got outside—and there, of all people waiting for her, was Melanie's young brother, Charles Hamilton, a sweet young boy supposed to be destined for Ashley's sister and with whom Scarlett had been flirting without mercy or thought all day, and all of which he had taken in dead earnest and fallen for completely—and now here he was excitedly telling her that word had just been received of declaration of war and call for volunteers and would Miss Scarlett marry him? Ah, that was an idea—she looked at him in a new light—here was the perfect means to her end—to show Ashley how little she cared— to hurt him and his sister and Melanie and the whole family— and all the other men. Besides, Charles was rich and lived in Atlanta—and why not? What matter if she didn't love him—

what matter anything, now that Ashley was lost? And thus was Charles transported to seventh heaven. . .

In 2 weeks, much to everyone's amazement, they were married—the day before Ashley's and Melanie's wedding. The effect of the war spirit was already upsetting this gentle orderly society—with weddings taking place on the heels of engagement announcements, instead of the traditional year's interval . . . But there was nothing that mothers and fathers could do about it with sons enlisted and marching off. Of course the war would only last a month. It wouldn't take long to teach those Yankees a lesson. But the adagio movement was becoming allegro . . . Days and nights were whirling past in a fever of excitement—of brave gay farewells, hectic preparations. And in the midst of it all Scarlett played the part of Charles' wife for a week—and then he was gone —and what was worse, Ashley was gone—all the young men were gone. This was what war meant to Scarlett—no men— nothing to do but wait for them to come back.

Two months later she was a widow—and expecting a baby. The word, expect, was slightly incongruous, for the last thing in the world that she had expected was a baby—and she certainly didn't want it—anymore than she had wanted Charles. Now a widow—and a mother—and seventeen. Why in heaven's name had she done such a thing—why had Ashley let her—why this ridiculous war—why did she have to sit around in deep mourning that meant nothing to her—sit around like an old lady—why this whole farce—when all she wanted to do was cut loose and have a good time as she always had. Mistaking her boredom and unhappiness for grief and shock, her parents sent her to visit all their relatives—that delightful Southern custom. As Miss Mitchell points out, Southerners have always been as enthusiastic visitors as hosts, and there was nothing unusual in relatives coming to spend the Christmas holidays and staying till July—of newly married couples going on a round of honeymoon visits and lingering in some pleasant home till the birth of their second child —of aunts and uncles and cousins coming to Sunday dinner and remaining till their burial years later. Scarlett, however, was back in no time. Traveling with a baby was no fun—and away, as at home, she had to act the part of the bereaved young widow who is through with life. Through with life?—why, she hadn't even begun.

Finally the answer came from—of all people—Melanie. That was hard to take, of course, but Scarlett was desperate. Melanie and her aunt wanted Scarlett and her baby to come and stay with them in Atlanta. Charles' little son should be in his father's home—and besides Melanie loved Scarlett—why, no one knew, least of all Scarlett. But Atlanta sounded attractive and there she went.

Immediately she loved it—this place suited her—it was as young and vital and vigorous and alive and lusty as she was—it was the new South—it was a town becoming a city—*the* city— overnight. Born of a railroad, now its railroads were connecting links between the eastern and western armies and the more southern bases of supplies. With all her ports blockaded, the agricultural South was forced into industry, into manufacturing, and Atlanta was trying to do it. It was a hospital base—it was everything—teeming with life and activity. The Hamilton home and the Hamilton prestige were wonderful. And, Melanie was so absurdly crazy about Scarlett's baby that she didn't have to bother much about him anymore. Best of all, there were men to be seen again.

True, she had to watch her step—not show too much interest —not seem to be enjoying herself—pretend that it was all for the Cause of the Confederacy. Only one person saw through her and delighted in it—and that was Rhett Bulter—Captain Rhett Bulter now—famous blockade-runner—one of the few men able to smuggle goods in and out—the goods they were beginning to need so badly—at first the luxuries, and then the necessities of food, clothes, medicine—and making a fortune at it. Rhett Butler knew she was no lady, yet never took advantage of it. Rhett Butler,—having a grand time out of the war as she was—who had no illusions about it—who said it was just a business, as all wars are—who dared say that the South didn't have a chance and was nearly killed for it—Rhett, who dared say all the things she thought and had been taught not to say—Rhett, the most exciting, exasperating, masculine man she ever knew—always one jump ahead of her—laughing at her—yet all gentleness and tenderness to her child and Melanie.

And the months become another year and Ashley returned on a brief furlough—and again Scarlett tried to take him away from Melanie in their own home—and again she failed. If she loved him, then she must promise to stay with Melanie—and take care of her in case anything happened. Miserably Scarlett promised. Anything—anything to show her love—

And then more months and all the light-hearted confidence and high-hearted hopes gone at Gettysburg—and a silent, grim courage in its place as the wounded poured in—men needing food and medicine and bandages no one had—food so scarce as to be priceless—the South dying, starving—and the sound of guns drawing nearer and nearer to Atlanta as the troops fall back in retreat. Railroads being cut off—people fleeing for their lives—a pall of gunfire over all. If only Scarlett could take her boy and leave—go home while there was yet time and some chance of getting there,—but no, she had promised Ashley to stay with Melanie who was going to have a baby and couldn't be moved. Scarlett stayed. And then Sherman's march to the sea—and the O'Hara plantation on that line of march—that trail of desolation —and no word—were they dead or alive? and Ashley reported missing—and then the siege of Atlanta begins and in the midst of it Melanie's baby is born—no doctor available—and Scarlett delivers it. As if by magic Rhett Butler appears—Rhett, who could have got away—who needn't be there—yet is there to save them—their wild flight with the two babies and Melanie and their frightened faithful darkies. Rhett escorts them to the outskirts—insures their safety—and then suddenly no longer the cynic but the Southerner, he returns to the siege.

The pages describing Scarlett's getting her little group of dependents back to the plantation—finding it in ruins—her mother dead—her father mad—her sisters sick with typhoid—the Negroes starving—how she rises to it all and manages to pull through—pull them all through is a story of heroic proportions. Relieved of the necessity of being a lady, now the woman in her can be set to work—to do a man's work—and more—to save this land—this home—these people who are her responsibility.

The war is over—but now there is what is fully as bad—the

Reconstruction Period—starting all over again from scratch—in poverty, ruins, against backbreaking, heartbreaking obstacles of military rule—of deprivation of all basic human rights—of insults and injustice—of being bled by the carpetbaggers and scalawags exploiting what little is left—and most pitiful of all: the Negroes miserable and bewildered in their freedom, without work, homes, the protection of the families of which they had been a part—the better class of them still clinging to their masters like children not knowing what to do in this strange new order of things, resenting what had been done to their masters and the rise of the white trash, scorning their lower brethren incited by liquor and propaganda and bribery to commit outrages they never would have otherwise. Slavery destroyed—to make way for the slave wage . . .

But the South bore its misfortunes as proudly as it had its fortune, and grimly set to work to save itself and some semblance of the old order. Some could not change, could not adjust themselves to the change and were lost. Among these was Ashley —returned from the war and prison camp a broken man, cherishing only his code of honor and tradition as a gentleman— even while at work in the fields of Scarlett's plantation—Ashley still the object of all Scarlett's dreams as she toiled for him and his family and her own—Scarlett carrying the burden of it all— fighting for their very existence—for some security—the fighter in her released from old conventions—released into the building of a new day and order—her own—the modern—more hardened than ever—more dedicated to only one purpose: to get money and power at any price—to be independent—to make a place for herself that could never again be taken away—the new post-war philosophy—like her own.

And when the plantation is threatened with confiscation through taxation, she does not hesitate. She makes a new dress out of some of her mother's old curtains, plucks a feather from the tail of their one rooster and goes to Atlanta to conquer Rhett Butler—Rhett the richest man in the South—the man who has always told her he will not marry—just the man to sell herself to for the price of the taxes. And so she makes him her offer—and he refuses. Why, we shall see later—as will she. But now she sees nothing—except pressing need and an end justifying any means, and in that mood she runs into elderly Frank Kennedy in the city, her sister's fiancé—Frank Kennedy, whom she has always ridiculed as a male old maid—Frank Kennedy, one of the few remaining men of the old families—now running a fairly profitable little grocery store—and she sets to work. She tells him her sister is untrue to him—and in 2 weeks Scarlett becomes Mrs. Frank Kennedy and has the money to send home to save the plantation.

And then, much to her husband's dismay, she sets to work reorganizing his little business—making him collect past due accounts he did not consider gentlemanly to press—and on top of that she borrowed money from Rhett Butler and bought a sawmill and went into the lumber business. Even in the bustling boom town of Atlanta rebuilding itself with frontier fever, Scarlett's modernity—her daring—created a sensation. For a lady to be a business woman—and a successful one—well, what was this new age coming to . . .?

Scarlett's next step was to bring Ashley and his family to Atlanta and put him in charge of her mill, where much to her surprise, she learned that his code of honor hampered him quite as much as a business man as it had as a lover. Worst of all, Melanie established herself in Atlanta society as Scarlett never had—or could. She was loved. And the thing no one could understand, least of all Scarlett herself, was the way Melanie loved Scarlett. Was she a fool not to see that all of Scarlett's interest was in Ashley? No, Melanie was not a fool—she was the rarest and loveliest of creatures—a true gentlewoman. She was constitutionally incapable of thinking evil of anyone. This was beyond Scarlett's comprehension completely. She resented Melanie's loyalty and devotion—her popularity—most of all the way in which she defended Scarlett socially. That this frail young woman lacking all her own physical power should have such a mental and moral force beyond it was a source of constant amazement and annoyance. Well, one good thing—the doctors had told Melanie she must never have another baby—and Scarlett took as much delight in that fact as dismay in the one that she was becoming a mother again. She wanted this child no more than her first. The first had interfered with her pleasure, and this one interfered with her business.

Unknown to their women at this time, the men of the South had organized themselves into a band known as the Ku Klux Klan. No one knew who belonged to it—only that it was made up of those who, unable to get any police protection, were taking the law into their own hands to combat the outrages to which they and their women were being exposed—a secret police force who did under cover of night what the Yankee police overlooked by day—It is interesting to note that this band was organized to resist persecution—and sad to reflect how it degenerated into an organization of persecution.

Scarlett had been constantly warned, begged and pleaded with not to go about the town alone so much—driving back and forth through the lone countryside to and from her mills— sections infested with ruffians of all sorts, the backwash of the war, reconstruction, etc. Finally one day it happened—she was attacked—and only her own Negro saved her. The news spread like wildfire—and that night all the men mysteriously disap- peared—and the Klan struck—cleaning up the countryside of its criminal element in one bloody raid. Immediately the police were out after the Klan—and to their fright every woman in Atlanta learned that her husband was suspect and under arrest. Only one person could save their lives for them—and did—Rhett Butler, who, through his hated and envied influential connections with the Yankee and Republican officials, was able to set them all free by swearing they had been with him at—of all places—a house of prostitution. This was a hard pill for Atlanta society to swallow . . . . And Rhett's eyes laughed more than ever.

But Frank Kennedy had been killed in the raid. Added to Scarlett's shock at all this was the uncomfortable realization that she had been the cause. Only two people stood by her—Melanie —and Rhett. Rhett did more than that—he married her.

Now she had reached the top—Mrs. Rhett Butler—the richest woman in the South—and Rhett sat back to watch her as he would a child to whom he had given toys to play with—the toys she had always wanted and struggled for. For the first time, Scarlett was married to a real man—a man she could not bully and dominate—a man who loved her with a passion she responded to for the first time in her life—responded to, but never saw the still greater depth of love that lay behind it waiting, watching for a similar love in her. Such things were beyond Scarlett's understanding, and he knew better than to try to teach her. Only life and time could do that. Their marriage was one of exhausting, exciting extremes—of ecstasies and agonies. Out of their ecstasy was born a child—the only one she ever wanted—and that child died. And in her selfishness she did not see Rhett's greater suffering. Only Melanie did. And then Melanie died. Upon Scarlett burst the realization that she had lost the only real friend she had ever had.

Now it has all turned out just as she hoped, prayed, dreamed, worked for—now she could have Ashley. Melanie is gone—Rhett is leaving her as he had married her—for her convenience—in too perfect understanding . . . . And suddenly all veils were lifted from her eyes—and the blind saw—saw that she didn't want Ashley Wilkes—that she had only wanted him when she couldn't get him—when it was a challenge—that the only two people who had ever really loved her and whom she loves are Melanie—lost to her through death—and Rhett—lost to her through her own blind selfishness and pig-headedness—her one friend—her one lover.

The one who had made the psychological mistake of letting her know she had loved her—the other strong enough, wise enough never to let her know how much he had loved her, knowing that it was only the unattainable that attracted her and held her interest, that her strength had outlet only in struggle for whatever was just beyond her reach. . . . Both—gone with the wind. And now there was a deadly calm. But—the wind would blow again. And Scarlett braced herself—to wait it out—an element against the elements—you can't say good—you can't say bad—anymore than you can of the wind itself that destroys life—but scatters the seeds for its survival—tomorrow . . .

Not too many years later the English poet Ernest Dowson wrote this line which will be better known now than ever before . . .

I have forgot much, Cynara! gone with the wind

Ethan Frome

By Edith Wharton

March 1976

The year 1975 brought us the definitive biography of one of America's major novelists—Edith Wharton—the first woman ever to be awarded the Pulitzer Prize. Prof. R.W.B. Lewis of Yale, who wrote this great biography, itself a Pulitzer Prize winner, realized that his subject was a life story as full of interest as any of Edith Wharton's novels.

As a novelist—and I urge you to go to the library and get and read her novels—she was a social historian for all the turn of the century and the first two decades of this century. All great novelists are the best of historians and psychologists; in addition, Mrs. Wharton was a complete realist. She did not choose to write of the erotic, but she could, as a story fragment among her private papers at Yale reveals in Lewis's biography.

From her birth into a family of New York wealth and aristocracy in 1862, until her death in 1937, her seventy-five years in New York, Massachusetts, and Europe covered all the transitions from Victoria to FDR and from Longfellow to Henry James to Sinclair Lewis to Kenneth Clark. Those years covered too the frustration of a miserable marriage and divorce, a couple of love affairs, a tremendous amount of travel and production of creative work, friendships with the most brilliant literary society here and abroad. For her great work for Belgian refugee children in World War I, she was given the Legion of Honor Award.

She lived in France for thirty years, but always in her short stories and novels she wrote of the New York and New England which had been her origin. In the novelette "Ethan Frome" she went beyond any personal origin and into the very roots of human drama. In short, she wrote a classic.

The book was first published in 1911, and no story has ever surpassed "Ethan Frome" in stark, simple, tragic power. And its power is perfectly concentrated in less than 200 pages.

We first meet Ethan Frome in a prologue. He is described as "a ruin of a man." Though still in early middle age, he is old— old as the grim ground he has struggled with all his life, old as the snows which have fallen upon it, as old and as silent. His face is a scarred mask, expressionless, the face of a man staring, not looking at a world in which he is more dead than alive. He walks with a painful limp. Literally a ruin of a man, a dark grotesque spectre against a background of earth buried in white winter, a vast barren desolation. Ethan Frome is a shattered spirit dragging a broken body to do the odd jobs left for shattered spirits and broken bodies to do to earn a dollar.

The Frome farmhouse is a ruin too—a coffin on *top* of the ground for those who are buried alive in snow, in silence, in solitude. Even if you have never been in New England you have seen such houses scattered through the wasteland stretches of our country—perhaps the adobe huts on our Southwest desert land— or the drab bunch of boards sticking up like scarecrows in the wilderness of really rural Texas, Oklahoma, Arkansas. . . . The only difference is that these bake under six months of scorching sun, and in the north they brood beneath six months of snow. Have you never wondered about what lives are lived in such houses, such isolation, as you go by on the highway or train and see a hand wave or just a figure standing, staring . . . ?

We go back to the Ethan Frome twenty years younger. We see a young man in the prime of physical strength, putting that strength without question or complaint into the acceptance and performance of the duties which were his lot and his life. It had not been much of a life except for those duties, the endless spinning of a web of circumstances. There had been one brief year in a technological school in Worcester. That was the only highlight. Then his father died, leaving him and his mother with a poverty-stricken farm, and soon she became a victim of melancholia.

The only things that sustained Ethan were his youth and strength. But at last even he reached the breaking point, and when cousin Zenobia Pierce came to help nurse his mother, she seemed like an angel. At least there was somebody to talk to—not much, for Zenobia's conversational powers were limited to the subject of symptoms in general and his mother's in particular— but it was better than nothing. Just the sound of another human voice can mean so much sometimes, even if what that voice says does not. Often that's why we switch on a radio or TV now when we're alone, just for an illusion of companionship. Of course Ethan had nothing like that, and so when his mother died and the prospect of being there entirely alone now was overwhelming, on an impulse of sheer desperation and some sense of obligation, he asked Zenobia to marry him. Winter had set in . . . perhaps if it had been spring? . . .

Immediately the strapping, robust Zenobia underwent an amazing change. After having been such an angel of efficiency when there had been someone to nurse, now she began just as efficiently to take the place of the patient left vacant by Ethan's unfortunate mother. Zenobia became vaguely sickly. Then she began developing that female wonder referred to as "complications."

In short, she was the sort of woman who enjoys sickness, her own or another person's. No more enduring portrait of a hypochondriac was ever given than here in Zenobia. Add selfishness, ignorance, coarseness, and downright meanness, and you get her picture in full dimension. You feel that she should have some measure of your pity, but for the life of you, you can't give her any. You can only feel sorry for everyone around her.

In sickness, as in everything else, there can be an art, and the tradition of an art. One of the basic ideals in us all is our admiration of courage. When a person is unfortunate, physically or otherwise, and is brave and uncomplaining, not as a conscious martyr but as a good soldier, our sympathy is deeply stirred. But when a person wallows in trouble, flaunts it, enjoys it, demanding and exploiting our sympathy, then we can feel only disgust and indifference. Zenobia loved poor health; it was her way of life. She set out to be the sickest woman in New England.

Her whine of complaints is the first sound that registers with us, for Ethan seldom speaks to answer unless she goads him to it. There just isn't anything to say. There hasn't been for seven years.

You get the picture—this drab, bleak shack of a farmhouse —Ethan silent and hardened by years of facing nothing but poverty, struggle, loneliness, and this rag, well-padded bones and hank of hair who only nags for more of the patent medicines he can't afford. And now the latest thing is that she must have a hired girl.

And so Mattie Silver enters the scene, a cousin of Zenobia's, a penniless orphan thankful for a roof over her head. Mattie is only twenty, a slip of a girl—her face the prettiest Ethan has ever seen because her eyes glow and her lips smile. For the first time there is laughter in this house, and a spark of human warmth.

Now Zenobia has a new victim, of course. She piles work on the girl and is never satisfied with the way it's done. But Mattie doesn't seem to mind this, and what annoys Zenobia even more is the way Ethan tries to make things easier for Mattie. He pities her for what she has to take from his wife and put up with, and we sense the understanding that grows between them.

Once a month Zenobia lets Mattie go into the village two miles away for the church sociable, so that nobody will think that she isn't doing her Christian duty for her cousin. On those nights Ethan is expected to walk to the village and escort her home. This duty is the most pleasant he's ever had.

He can talk and share his thoughts with Mattie. Ethan was not an ignorant yokel. He was a man sensitive to beauty, eager for knowledge, starved for companionship. And now there was this girl stepping along so joyously beside him, listening so raptly to all he said, chattering back so gaily—Mattie who thought he was God and made him feel as if he were.

They are in love with each other, deeply, passionately, hungrily, hopelessly—and innocently. Yes, *innocently,* for neither of them ever even speaks of it. All their background and tradition, the Puritan Code, stands between them just as if Zenobia herself were walking there between them. No, they do not speak of love. But, as you and I know, one does not have to speak of love. Love speaks for itself in all the many different ways which those who love always understand, perhaps a look, a chance touch of the hand . . .

And so Ethan and Mattie knew, and so intense was their love and need that they created a tension just in trying to conceal it. They should not, they could not love each other. Then why did they? How many times has that question been asked—and left unanswered?

Gradually Zenobia develops a new symptom. Suspicion. These two persons around her seem to be happy, and that can't be right. Besides, Ethan is shaving three times a week now. You see, their very innocence betrays them.

From her bottles and blankets Zenobia rises on what she assures them are her last legs and goes into town to see a new doctor. She will be gone over night because of the snow.

And so Ethan and Mattie are left alone together—scared to death—and intoxicated with happiness. The pathos of that happiness is unforgettable, as they try to make-believe, and then fearfully say goodnight to each other at nine o'clock just as usual, just as if Zenobia was there.

Her return next day was cheerful, for the trip has been a success. The new doctor had found her much worse than any doctor before. Now she must have a real hired girl to do everything, and what's more she has already engaged one. Of course she doesn't expect Ethan to keep Mattie too. Mattie is to go—and good riddance.

At first Ethan could say nothing. This was too horrible a thing even for Zenobia to do. And then all the long pent-up emotion burst out of him in rage. He was making his one fight, not only for his love, but for his life.

Mattie has nothing and no place to go. What will she do? He will go with her. He will make the break at last and get away from Zenobia and the farm, all his bondage and slavery. But then the Puritan character, the Puritan conscience, the Puritan mind with its dedication to duty assert themselves. Ethan faces the facts. How can he go? How could he take care of Mattie? Where is the money? Borrow it? Would any of the village people loan him money to desert his wife, his duty? No chance of that. He is caught worse than any mouse in any trap. He can do nothing that will not appear mad, wild, wrong, all wrong. Desperately he and Mattie stand together in defeat.

Once again they are on the snowcovered hillside where they have so often stopped to talk. But now the words come that were never spoken before, as they face the hopelessness of a future blank without each other. They have had nothing, but at least they have had that nothing together. And so the Puritan breaks at last. In a frenzy the idea comes—to take that slide down the hill now—and not come up again. They will head the sled straight into the big elm tree at the bottom—it will be over in a minute—a second. If they cannot live together, they can at least die together. They huddle together on the sled—there's a rush of wind—they are off—over the hilltop and down—to escape—to peace—to Liebestod. . . . And it seems we can hear the sound of the sled bounding away faster and faster. . . .

Twenty years later and the scene of the real tragedy, for they did not die. They live. Ethan, the ruin of a man. Mattie, half-mad ruin of a woman, babbling like a baby in a wheel-chair. And Zenobia, miraculously restored to health, doctoring, caring for them both.

They live. They are doomed to live . . . these three together. They will always live in this book and with you who read it.

For just a moment more, let's stay together, think together about something we hear so often asked—the question why almost all of the great books are tragic. For it is true. They are. And briefly here's the reason why . . .

Great art, whatever else it is or isn't according to the countless definitions, is that which stirs and moves us, means something to us, not just to one person at one time, but to all persons in all times. Now what are the things that affect us all most deeply? They are the tragic things in life—the crucial sorrows, separations, frustrations, the disappointments which we all experience. These are the things that make us one. We do not all laugh at the same things. But we all cry together. In sorrow we are brothers. Laughter comes from the head, the nervous system. But tears come from the heart. And great art is written in tears, the language we all understand.

So few of us ever get what we want, and if we do, it is ours for only a little while. We get it but to lose it. And all of this is natural, is life. But there is also something else in us that dares to hope and dream and desire. And when this irresistible force meets that immovable object in words or music or any form of our expression, then we have Art, because we have Life and the strange, compelling, mystic beauty of the Truth about Life.

Think over the great books, the great plays, poems, love stories in words and in music. . . . They are all tragedies.

Comedy is an escape from life. Tragedy faces it. And it is interesting too that the only comedies which endure as art are either fantasies or satires. Think this over and see if it isn't so.

This is the answer to our question. Not from me, but from the Book of Life which you can review as well as I.

The Glass Menagerie

By Tennessee Williams

November 1945

One play has been outstanding in 1945 on the Broadway stage, and that play of course is "The Glass Menagerie." But it is not only a play to be seen—it is drama to be read as literature because that is what it is most essentially, and that is why it is important to all of us whose interest is in the literature of our time.

I could talk for a long while about the technique of this man Tennessee Williams and of his play in comparative analysis with the work of other literary dramatists such as Shaw, O'Neill, Thornton Wilder, William Saroyan, Clifford Odets, Lillian Hellman, Maxwell Anderson, etc.—and though I could and would show you how and why this play is important, it can speak for itself to you. But until you get a copy and come into direct contact with the fine thought and writing which have gone into its dialogue and characterization and commentary, let me raise the curtain on the first scene of "The Glass Menagerie."

Out of Tom Wingfield's memory it emerges—that scene of home in St. Louis in 1930—that apartment facing an alley in the back of a typical big city apartment house. The time is back in the 1930's when, as Tom says, "The huge middle class of America was matriculating in a school for the blind."

Tom is a young man with the eyes of a poet—and he works in a warehouse—because he has to. We see his sister Laura, a lovely girl with eyes as sensitive as his own. Left crippled from a childhood illness, one leg is held in a brace. Her greatest treasure is her collection of lovely little glass figures of animals in

83

miniature that reflect the same delicacy that is herself. Laura has never been able to have and do the things that other girls her age have and do, and so there is that wistfulness about her, an air of a life dreamed instead of lived. And then there is their mother Amanda, and when we come to Amanda we have to stop a minute, because here is a character who seems too simple not to be complex.

Amanda Wingfield is still a very pretty woman who has never gotten over the fact that she was a beautiful girl—and a very popular one. Indeed, her chief trouble is that she is determined to live in the illusion that she still is that girl. This makes her rather foolish and silly and sometimes pathetic and yet not unattractive if you are not around her long enough to have it get on your nerves. And because she refuses to face the facts of life she makes life not only unpleasant but painful for those who know and want the reality of their own lives. In other words she is one of those persons who "means well," but means to have her own way—and in a parent that can be a pretty vicious thing. Her own life has been a failure and she is trying desperately to redeem that failure through her children, as so many parents do. The possibility that her own sense of values might be wrong, as wrong for her children as for herself, is a thought that has never occurred to her. She sees herself only as a victim of circumstances—just a girl who was led to the altar by the wrong man.

All that is left of that man now is a picture. There are times when his children envy him. As Toms says, "Father was a telephone man who fell in love with long distances and gave up his job to skip the light fantastic out of town a long time ago. The last we heard of him was a postcard from Mexico with two words on it—hello—goodbye—and no address." And so that is all we know of Mr. Wingfield—except that he must have been a man of considerable courage.

Amanda simply refuses to believe that a daughter of hers cannot be the sort of person she wants her to be. And so every evening she goes on talking, playfully pretending that some man must be on his way to come to see Laura, fall desperately in love with her, have a great romance and a most successful marriage— all this despite the fact that Laura does not have any friends, boy or girl. Of course Amanda means to give her confidence, but the effect is just the opposite, for it only makes Laura more conscious of her loneliness, her sense of failure, defeat and inferiority.

There they are—mother and daughter living together and loving each other, and yet Amanda has no more understanding of the real nature and needs of her child than if they were complete strangers. Only Tom knows, and he is helpless because he is caught in the same trap and suffers from the same misunderstanding, all in the name of mother-love. And so there is nothing to do but let mother talk—or get out. Tom gets out as soon as possible every night. But Laura can't.

In the next scene when Amanda comes in you know that something has happened and is going to happen. Laura knows it too and we can feel her fear as she tries to make it appear to her mother that she has been working at her typewriting lesson instead of her glass collection. But Amanda who has gone out to attend her beloved D.A.R. meeting had stopped by the business school and found out that Laura had not been attending her class at all. Just where has she been all the time she was supposed to have been there? Hesitantly, fearfully Laura explains that she had been out walking—the art museum and the flower gardens in the park—anything anywhere to escape that typewriting and shorthand class—can't her mother see and understand how and why she can't do it—that everything in her rebels against it and that no matter how much she wants to be an obedient daughter she can't make herself do this thing—she can't make herself into something that she isn't.

All this is lost on Amanda who can only see and say that if a girl won't get herself married or learn to be a stenographer there is just nothing to save her from starvation. The Lord knows she is trying to do her best as a mother, but what can she do with children who don't cooperate with her and appreciate it?

In the next scene that night there is another explosion, this time with Tom. He is trying to do some writing, and his mother interrupts him as she always does and begins nagging at him about wasting his time like this and reading awful books he brings home—like the one by that Mr. D.H. Lawrence which she simply won't allow in the house—and she *knows* that when he goes out every night to the movies he is not always going to the movies—nobody could go to the movies that much—and where is it that he does go and stay out so late that he doesn't get nearly enough sleep to make a success of his job—how can he be so selfish when he knows they must depend on him?

Well, Tom stands all of this that he can and then his nerves snap and he lets her have it. The pity of it is that he does go to the movies—where else can he go on sixty-five dollars a month when that sixty-five dollars a month must support them all and he sacrifices everything in life that he cares anything about—no time to read and write and think and just be to himself—yes, he goes to the movies just to get away from home and try to get away from himself, the self that isn't himself at all—he goes to the movies, yes, to try to get vicariously a little of the adventure he has always dreamed of and never had in his own life—yes, the pity of it is that he does go to the movies just to escape—this.

Of course his mother doesn't understand anything he is talking about. Why can't there be enough adventure in a good job at a warehouse for any young man of ambition if he works hard to get ahead and make something out of himself? And so one word leads to another of course and both of them say things that hurt, and finally in a fury of desperation Tom jumps up and pulls on his coat to leave, but he can't get into it fast enough to get out and away from her and he throws the coat across the room and starts to run out—and the coat lands against the cabinet that holds Laura's beloved glass collection and shatters it. At his sister's cry, Tom comes back and sadly begins picking up the pieces.

Amanda won't speak to her son after that until he apologizes to her for what he said, and finally Laura prevails upon him to do it. Then as soon as her pride is restored and Amanda can begin talking to him, she tells him that he's just got to help her get Laura away from that ridiculous glass menagerie and playing phonograph records all the time and instead meet—a *man*. Surely there must be some nice fellow at the warehouse—one who doesn't drink—he simply *must* not drink—whom Tom can bring home to meet his sister and then let Nature take its course as Amanda is convinced that there can be only one course for Nature to take.

The awful obviousness of this is as revolting to Tom as he

knows it would be painful to Laura, but to please his mother he finally agrees. And a few evenings later he tells her that he has asked a fellow by the name of Jim O'Connor to come over for dinner tomorrow night. If he had told Amanda that he was bringing home a million dollars she couldn't have been more excited. This is her dream come true—a man coming to see Laura—and it doesn't bother her at all when Tom points out that men and women can meet each other and often do without anything quite as violent as marriage as an immediate necessity. But Amanda isn't even listening to him—all she wants to know is what this Jim O'Connor does—a shipping clerk at eighty-five dollars a month—well, that's all right to start with—and he goes to night school—why, that's wonderful and shows he has ambition—now how can she get everything ready by tomorrow—a new dress for Laura—just the right things for dinner—Friday and O'Connor will mean fish—and clean the house and get out and polish the silver—and make everything ready for Prince Charming.

In the next scene, though it's the same scene you'd hardly know the place. Amanda has worked like mad and the little apartment looks like new. And Laura has on a new dress and is scared to death. She can't understand all this fuss, and then when she does it frightens her more, for she knows she can't be and do what her mother expects of her. Besides it just so happens that Jim O'Connor was the one boy in high school she always loved. Of course he never knew it—nobody knew it—he was so popular —led the glee club, the debating team, the basketball team, and she just used to sit in class and look at him—look and love—and now how can she meet him like this again?

Understanding nothing of the psychology of this sensitive child's nature, Amanda is radiant with what seems to her such additional romance—the reunion of childhood sweethearts, the triumph of true love. As a matter of fact she looks even younger than Laura tonight—dressed in the gown she wore to lead the cotillion at the governor's ball that fatal night when she met her husband.

When the doorbell rang she has to force Laura to answer it, for the girl is so nervously sick and weak. Tom and Jim come in

—and Jim doesn't even recognize Laura. She runs into the kitchen and Amanda hastens to explain it's because she's so domestic.

Jim O'Connor is one of those big fellows who give promise in the high school years that nothing can stop them from becoming President of the United States. And then after that something happens—instead of going and growing on, some sort of paralysis sets in and they stay just as and what and where they were—and nothing happens at all—they reached their limit just when it seemed they had none. The result is that you remember him as the eternal president of the senior class—and wonder what's become of him?

After dinner of course Amanda sends Jim to sit with Laura and keeps Tom out in the kitchen to help with the dishes. And so at last the climax is here—the moment so desperately arranged—Laura is alone with her first gentleman caller—and it's Jim, the only one she ever dreamed of.

They begin talking, or rather he does—and gradually he draws her out of her shell of shyness and fear—and then he kisses her—and it is as if new life comes into her, as if she becomes alive for the first time, and it's a new Laura we see before us. Then he tells her that he has to leave early now and go because he has to meet a train, the train his girl is coming in on—the girl he's engaged to marry.

When he says that, it is as if we can almost hear the shattering of glass, those little pieces as fragile as the dream just born in this girl's heart and now still-born. The precious moment of communion is over. The Prince is gone without knowing that he might have been a Prince. And the Princess is back in her tower alone with this one memory to add to her collection of dreams.

When Amanda discovers what has happened—that after all this preparation and effort and expense Tom brought home a man engaged to be married,—her disappointment makes her furious. How could Tom be so stupid as not to have known a thing like that when so much depended on it? And again one word leads to another in the storm of hate that destroys all hope of love where there is no understanding. No greater hurt, no deeper injury to the spirit can be inflicted than between those whose love is without understanding, who are of one flesh and blood but speak a different language and are forever strangers.

And so it was that Tom left home as his father had before him—because there was no home, really. Whose fault was that? The obvious answer of course is that it was Amanda. And yet that wasn't so, for she was just as much a victim of it all as her husband and children. It was just that none of them belonged together, except Tom and Laura. And that wasn't because they were brother and sister but because the poet in him understood the mystic in her. Together they could have been happy. There are Tom's words just before the curtain falls: "I went away—far away—for time is the longest distance between two places. I was fired for writing a poem on the lid of a shoe box. I left St. Louis. I traveled. The cities swept about me like dead leaves, leaves brightly colored but torn away from the branches. I would have stopped, but I was pursued by something. It always came upon me unawares, taking me altogether by surprise. Perhaps it was a bit of music. Perhaps a piece of transparent glass. Perhaps I was walking along a street at night in some strange city before I have found companions. I pass the lighted window of a shop where perfume is sold. The window is filled with pieces of colored glass, tiny transparent bottles in delicate colors, like bits of shattered rainbow. Then all at once my sister touches my shoulder. I turn around and look into her eyes. Oh Laura, Laura, I tried to leave you behind me, but I am more faithful than I intended to be! I reach for a cigarette, I cross the street, I run into the movies or a bar, I buy a drink, I speak to the nearest stranger—anything to forget what could not be."

Love and care and opportunity and understanding and guidance are what children need and naturally turn to mothers and fathers for,—but each child that is born is a person, a separate individual who must find and follow his own destiny for happiness. That is his right as a human being—the right to the chance to be himself and learn from his own mistakes, not yours. To interfere with that right results in the worst tragedies we know,—people waiting forever for the gentleman caller who is symbolic of an experience of fulfillment which they have been led to expect from life instead of finding for themselves in their own life.

"The Glass Menagerie" is more than theater—it is a poet's deep and discerning commentary on the vital drama of human psychology in all homes that are not homes and where the little things that shape our lives and cripple the spirit can have such devastating effect from generation to generation. And the symbolism of glass, of lives lived in miniature and reflection, is apt, for only one thing breaks more easily—and that of course is the human heart.

To me one of the most significant speeches that Mr. Williams puts into the mouth of Tom Wingfield is that it is the frustration in the lives of so many people that makes war a welcome adventure—giving the little man the illusion of a chance to break out of his trap of routine and become the focus of attention and importance for a while, however short a while.

The Rise and Fall of the Third Reich

By William Shirer

October 1960

In the field of non-fiction, and without any question, here is the book of greatest importance to come to us this year—"The Rise and Fall of the Third Reich, A History of Nazi Germany." The author is the American who knew more about it than any other man. In fact, he was the first person to report and warn us of what had evolved, was happening and would happen there. He did that early in 1941 in his book "Berlin Diary." William Shirer.

Thirty years of personal experience and research, plus five years of writing, have been put into this new book by Mr. Shirer. The result is the most expert, readable and vital of any contemporary history. It is worth every penny of its ten dollar price, nor will this price keep it from being a bestseller.

This complete history of Nazi Germany, complete even to a last minute footnote on the capture of Eichmann, could not come to us at a better time in order to warn us again—for now with our attention focused on Russia, we are distracted from this other enemy still very much present and active just below the surface in Western Germany. Enemies like that do not become friends in a short span of fifteen years. To read this history of barely a generation ago is to be forcibly reminded of the fatal foolishness of forgetting. As Shirer quotes from the great Santayana, "Those who do not remember the past are condemned to relive it."

When you get this book, as you will because you cannot afford to miss it, begin by looking at the map inside the front cover—the map shows just how far the Nazi conquest went over Europe and into Africa. Then don't miss Mr. Shirer's introduction, in which he explains why it is unnecessary to wait until a later time and a longer perspective in order to write this history. The reason is very simple—for when Hitler's empire fell there never was so much documentary evidence immediately available. In fact the U.S. First Army captured almost five hundred tons of German government records, and that was only a drop in the bucket.

Then came the fifty-two volumes of testimony at the Nuremberg Trials—plus all the reports of survivors of the concentration camps—and the egomania of Nazi leaders which overflowed into diaries.

No, there was no need, as Shirer says, to wait any longer to write this history. No amount of perspective could alter the documentary facts in this case.

Now it all comes out—all the fantastic details we never knew, we who consider ourselves a well-informed people. The intrigues with Russia when Hitler and Stalin had their heads together over the champagne glasses—the plans to exterminate the English people—the melodramatic plot to kidnap the Duke and Duchess of Windsor—the sex mania and insanity which took outlet in anti-Semitism—and perhaps most important of all: the background analysis of the German national psychology which is not a thing that changes, is changed, or has changed . . . I can only tell you that you read through these pages with Mr. Shirer with your eyes popping, as you see and hear what was recorded by secretaries and stenographers who never thought that such things would ever get out—to us.

One of many shocking little eye-openers is the fact that tons of German records were brought over here after the war, stored in a Virginia warehouse, and never were opened and examined before our government was ready to ship them back to Germany —still intact and unread. Only the interest and action of the American Historical Association and a couple of private foundations donating staff and equipment were responsible for having them checked and photostated.

To read of the many times Hitler bluffed his way to power when his own generals were scared to death that the bluff would be called and the Allies would begin to fight—times when one battle, one air raid would have stopped him—to see all that the policy of appeasement let develop, step by step, simply repudiates common sense—and only twenty years after the First World War.

This is what alerts us now to wonder at what these months and years are shaping—and on a much more shrunken map today.

To the best of my judgement and in the limited time of this program, I would say this—if you read only one book of nonfiction this year, let it be "The Rise and Fall of the Third Reich," William Shirer's History of Nazi Germany which in 1933 Hitler said would last a thousand years. It did last twelve years and four months—long enough to take everything from the Atlantic to the Volga and from the North Cape to the Mediterranean—and to destroy more millions of non-military people than ever before in history.

Many books have been written on special aspects and phases, events and effects—but here for the first time is the whole and complete story in the clear, simple words of a man who did not have to wait until everything was over in order to know what had happened—and how and why.

The Origin, A Novel of Charles Darwin

By Irving Stone

September 1980

Since 1934 when Irving Stone created the literary art form of the biographical novel and generated its instant popularity with the life story of Vincent Van Gogh in *Lust for Life*, we have enjoyed a rich series of books from him that have revitalized history and brought men and women of special interest back to life as if we were contemporaries.

Do you remember (and if you don't, just go and get them, for all his books are kept in print) *Immortal Wife* (Jessie Fremont), *Love Is Eternal* (Mary Lincoln), *The President's Lady* (Rachel Jackson), *Those Who Love* (Abigal Adams), *The Agony and the Ecstasy* (Michelangelo), *Passions of the Mind* (Sigmund Freud), *The Greek Treasure* (Henry and Sophia Schliemann)? To that roster of achievement his prodigal production includes the history *Men to Match My Mountains* and memorable biographies of Jack London and Clarence Darrow. Nor is this list complete. Always the Irving Stone subjects have been the men or women who reached both heights and depths in living with the mystery of themselves and the challenges of their times.

Now after his usual years of meticulous research with his editor-wife, Jean Stone, he has given us the summation of his skill and talent as historian-novelist in this new book *The Origin,* the life story of Charles Darwin.

It's an interesting coincidence that it was published only a matter of months after the British Broadcasting Co. and Time-Life's television production *The Voyage of Charles Darwin* was aired over our Public Broadcasting System. What was capsuled and transient on the screen is now in full dimension and forever in our hands, as only a book can be.

Irving Stone has us meet young Charles Darwin at the beautiful family home called The Mount in Shrewsbury, just after his graduation in theology at Cambridge. Not handsome, but goodlooking with his red hair, brown eyes that looked at everything so keenly, a gentle manner. Now in 1831 he was twenty-two, tall, athletic as an expert rider, hunter, hiker. Perhaps the most notable thing about him was his ease with people. They liked him, even if they couldn't understand why he was always collecting beetles. All the world of nature fascinated him—a rock, a bird, an insect, a flower, a tree, reptile, fish, animal, man.

The Darwins were a loving family. The only shadow on their home life had been Mrs. Darwin's death when Charles was a child. She had been of the wealthy Wedgwood family, the noted makers of pottery and china, and the two families remained very close with each other.

Dr. Darwin had a high reputation in the medical profession, and even his three hundred pounds weight seemed to inspire confidence in patients instead of dismay—which shows how our thinking changes. He had hoped, of course, that his two sons would become doctors. Neither did, but if Charles was going to doctor souls, that was acceptable.

Science had had a hard time at Cambridge because of religious prejudice against it, but gradually the natural sciences of botany and geology were tolerated, and those professors were Charles' most cherished friends. In fact, he was getting ready now to go with the geologist on a field trip into the mountains of Wales.

It was when he returned home from that trip that the letter came from the botany professor—the letter of destiny—the offer to go as naturalist on a Royal Navy ship commanded by Captain Robert Fitzroy to survey the southern coast of South America, Tierra del Fuego—a two-year voyage returning via the South Sea Islands and East Indies.

Charles could hardly believe his eyes. It was like a dream—the chance to see so much of the world and to work with what he knew now he loved best—the study of nature. Now all those hours he had spent in secret study at the museums and libraries in

Edinburgh and Cambridge away from his regular classes were to be fulfilled. Now he knew that he was about to find himself and his profession—that he had his foot on the bottom rung of the ladder of science—botany, geology, biology, zoology. . . .

The family were torn between pride and their fear of such a long separation and the dangers of the voyage. His father had to come to see that Charles was not drifting from one thing to another but was on a course with a solid, practical, respectable future, and it was the Wedgwood side of the family who most encouraged it, young cousin Emma and her father.

And so in a flurry of excitement and fond farewells, Charles packed his carefully selected books and instruments and clothes and was off to London to meet Capt. Fitzroy and then on to Plymouth to see the ship that held his fate—the H.M.S. *Beagle*. There were also new orders to add surveys of the west coast of South America and to cross the Pacific to Australia and New Zealand and across the Indian Ocean and around the Cape of Africa. The voyage would be at least four years instead of two. England was keeping her command of the seas and her navy busy charting the seaways for more and more trade.

Charles absorbed the shock of this latest information. He liked the captain, though he sensed the man's eccentricity. It would be an interesting companionship to be more severely tested by time than he knew.

After much delay from bad weather, they set sail two days after Christmas in that year of 1831. The great voyage was begun —and so was Charles Darwin's misery with seasickness.

There's an excellent map in the book which you can follow easily as you live almost every day with these men and crew whom you come to know so well in the close confinement of that ship—sharing the awesome storms—the overwhelming wonders of the tropics, their shores and forests teeming with plant and animal life, the shells and rocks and fossils—the insects, reptiles, birds, plants, as Darwin collects what no museum ever saw before. We look and see through his eyes, feel through his fingers and hands, open our minds with his to new thinking to displace and then replace old theories about our earth and world—new answers, at first hesitant and then confident, to old questions about How and Why and When and Where.

With him too we meet the natives and colonists on all the inland adventures, and at every possible port he crates and ships his cargo of evidence home to England and Cambridge, his notes and letters describing everything. On every page we feel the human warmth of this man, the drive of his dedication, the budding and then flowering courage of the secrets he confides in his diary and journal as he becomes more and more aware of the storm that this material will arouse among all who take the Biblical story of creation literally. To him there is no conflict, for he sees God as creator of the very laws he is discovering, laws that govern the processes of nature.

Step by step we move with him along the way whether on shipboard, on horseback, on foot, as the seasons and thousands of miles pass and the calendar is turned. Hungrily we wait with him for the letters from home, months apart—the personal news and then the congratulations of the professors already hailing him as one of the world's leading naturalists, both in science and philosophy. But the young man who is aging through these five years is more humble than ever.

The climax came in the Galapagos Islands as the variation in the tortoises and finch birds unlocked and opened the last door to his study of the origin of species. In his mind's eye was the vast scenery now of a whole new world of knowledge, and his heart had the palpitations that warned him of the stress being put on his own body.

The return home was utter euphoria. The family were beside themselves with joy. Reunion with his colleagues at Cambridge had a special excitement, but it was hard for Darwin to understand that they considered him their leader now and that he was famous.

His collections were the pride and talk of the museums. They rushed him into publication and lectures and the officialdom of all the major scientific societies. It was in the midst of all that when he began to realize something very vital—he was in love with the dear cousin who had always believed in him—Emma Wedgwood. Now at last he was ready for marriage. He proposed, and to her it was a dream come true. They were married in

January 1839 and moved to London where he should be for all that he had to do.

Honors poured in upon him and his work—until in 1859 he gave in to pressure and allowed his *Origin of Species* to be published. His own plan had been to leave it for posthumous publication.

At once the flood of fanatic disapproval broke upon him with charges of blasphemy, despite the acclaim of most of the scientific world.

Twelve hundred and fifty copies were printed in that first edition and sold out so fast that edition after edition were rushed into print with translation all over Europe.

As the religious controversy raged, friends such as Thomas Huxley rallied around him. He needed their support as well as the devotion of his family, because his health was breaking. Illness, not criticism, was his worry. There was still so much to do —more books to shed the light on so many facets that he was gifted to see.

Forever opposed to slavery, he was furious with the London *Times* support of the South in the American Civil War.

Darwin was never knighted by Queen Victoria. The government was afraid to allow that. But when at last death came in April 1882, England insisted that he be buried in Westminster Abbey—and just a few feet from Sir Isaac Newton.

Because of a request he left, no inscription was put upon the tomb—only the name Charles Robert Darwin and the dates of birth and death. He had always written simply, so that all could understand. This then was the ultimate simplicity of his greatness.

Darwin had wanted to come to the United States. Now he has, thanks to Irving Stone.

The Old Man and the Sea

By Ernest Hemingway

September 1952

In July, 1898, in Oak Park, Illinois, a young doctor and his wife by the name of Hemingway had a son they named Ernest. They moved to Michigan where the boy went to school, played football, went in for boxing, tennis, and fishing. An altogether normal, healthy life and he grew into a tall, goodlooking fellow with a mustache as soon as that was possible.

After school he got a job as reporter on the Kansas City *Star*. Then before America entered the war, he served as a volunteer ambulance driver in France and later enlisted in the Italian army. For his heroism he received a serious shoulder injury and all the medals Italy could give him. After the war he came home, married, returned to newspaper work and was sent to Europe as special correspondent for William Randolph Hearst in Paris. At twenty-five he was a success. He was writing short stories and poems and whenever possible he was fishing or attending bull fights.

Then his books began—in 1926 "The Sun Also Rises"—a year later "Men Without Women"—in 1929 "A Farewell to Arms"—1932 "Death in the Afternoon"—1935 "Green Hills of Africa"—1937 "To Have and Have Not"—1940 "For Whom the Bell Tolls"—1950 "Across the River and Into the Trees"—and now one of his best pieces of work I think—this classic of a novelette "The Old Man and the Sea."

What makes this man and his work so important that a book of only 140 pages is a literary event?

Because 140 pages of Hemingway are equal and superior to

1400 pages of many another writer—so stripped to the bone of condensed simplicity are his art and style. And because his writing has had the greatest influence on our literature for a quarter of a century now.

"The lost generation" Gertrude Stein called the writers after the First World War, and that was just about the most sensible thing she ever said. Lost, they were. Not materially, for success came fast—too quickly in the case of F. Scott Fitzgerald. But when and whenever the whole world sets out to destroy itself,— thinking men, creative artists, lose their faith in everything that went before and led up to such destruction. Distrusting the past, they have to find their own way through the present and into the future. They think it's a new way, but they soon find it leads to the time-tested scale of values and that it was never the moral law that failed us—but only we who failed it.

Ernest Hemingway, more than any other writer and whether you like it or not, set the pattern for most of all our contemporary fiction. Rejecting all patterns himself as a complete individualist, he has been imitated by the majority of all authors writing today.

Of course the modern way was paved by men like Theodore Dreiser, Sherwood Anderson, and Carl Sandburg, who in turn carried forward the idea of writing about life realistically from men like Flaubert and his colleagues in France.

The idea was to turn your back on romance in life, philosophy, art, literature. So many big and beautiful words like "Democracy" and "Christianity" had been used and abused in the politics of war as to lose all meaning for the young men who suffered through it. Carl Sandburg had already said "Look out how you use proud words. When you let proud words go, it is not easy to call them back." Later in "The Sun Also Rises" Hemingway was to have one of his characters say "You lose it if you talk about it." Meanings were to be found and defined only in action. Truth was not at home in elaborate and pretty speeches. Words were not to be wasted. They must be written as they are spoken by people close to the fundamental of life which, as Hemingway sees it, is death—and the fear and danger of death or courage to meet it.

In "A Farewell to Arms" he has one of the men say "I am

embarrassed by the words *sacred, glorious, sacrifice*. We have heard them and read them over and over for a long, long time, and I have seen nothing sacred and the things that were glorious had no glory and the sacrifices were like the stockyards at Chicago. There are many words I cannot bear to hear. Only the names of places have dignity."

This economy of simple words, staccato sentences, the common speech of the common man in whatever class, race or nationality of society, is the Hemingway style, as it is with Steinbeck. It looks simple and easy, but it is not when it's effective. A rigid discipline of skill and technique is involved in this sort of literary art—when it is an art—to express a profound thought or any beauty with only a minimum of all the keyboard of language.

Certainly few of us, including myself, care to see our literature reduced to nothing but this style. Most of us cherish beauty in writing and enjoy all the beauty in language we can get, but that doesn't keep us from appreciating what a Hemingway has to offer. In fact he himself removed many of his self-imposed limitations of style in "For Whom the Bell Tolls," even using the Biblical "thee" and "thou" for his lovers in their talk with each other. And of course the whole subject of that book was the social conscience in man and in himself that gradually evolved in Hemingway through the years as he became convinced of two, to him, basic values of positive, real, and enduring force in life— man's courage and man's love. They end his search for the truth. They begin his religion. It is not a bad ending or beginning.

Here are a few things he has said along the way—"People write when there is nothing to say, no water in the well" . . . "What I want is to write as well as I can and learn as I go along. I am interested in other things. I have a good life but I must write a certain amount or I do not enjoy the rest of my life which is a damned good life" . . . "The great thing is to last and get your work done and see and hear and understand; and write when there is something you know; and not before; and not too damned much after. Let those who want to save the world if you can get to see it clear and whole" . . . "Prose is much more difficult to write than poetry. There is a prose that has never been written.

There is a fourth and fifth dimension if anyone is serious enough and has luck. But it must be written without tricks and without cheating. With nothing that will go bad afterwards."

There we come, through his ideal of writing, to this man's idea of morality. We find it in his "Death in the Afternoon"—"I know only that what is moral is what you feel good after." And in "The Sun Also Rises"—"Immorality is what makes you disgusted afterwards." The very simplicity of these words might be misleading if you don't stop to think them over, for they are loaded with meaning, and the meaning reaches all the way back to the Ten Commandments.

Sometimes as we begin reading Hemingway novels and stories, we find ourselves wondering—"why am I reading about such characters—coarse, crude, common—indifferent, insensitive to all our standards?" But as we go on, we come to see that they *are* concerned with what is good or bad—only they must find it out for themselves.

So too when Hemingway comes to love, as finally in "A Farewell to Arms" this is said, "When you love you wish to do things for. You wish to sacrifice for. You wish to serve. You cannot know about it unless you have it." And later in "For Whom the Bell Tolls" as Robert Jordan is thinking to himself about his love for Maria come these words: "What you have with Maria, whether it lasts just through to-day and to-morrow or for a long life is the most important thing that can happen to a human being."

These are not the thoughts or words of a cynic but of someone thinking through with a seemingly childlike logic to truth gained step by step.

Nothing could demonstrate all this better than his new story —"The Old Man and the Sea."

The scene is a little fishing village, Cuba, and there are two characters—a very old fisherman by the name of Santiago and a very young boy whose name is Manolin. They are friends who love each other as dearly as only a great teacher and devoted pupil can, for the old man has taught the boy all that he knows about fishing for the great fish in the Gulf Stream—and that is a very great deal, for there is no older, finer fisherman in Cuba than

Santiago—even if he has gone 84 days now without catching one of the big fish.

Santiago lived and fished alone. Only Manolin came to his shack or went out in his boat with him. But now Manolin had to go in another boat because his father said that the old man was unlucky and a failure. It was a very unhappy separation for both of them, and it was hard to tell which one missed the other more.

Each day when the fishermen came home and the successful ones sold their huge marlin at the fish house to be trucked in ice to the market in Havana—or their sharks to the shark factory on the other side of the cove—Manolin was waiting to meet the old man and help him care for his empty boat and carry the harpoon and sail and heavy lines up to his empty shack.

And now that Manolin was making money fishing in a lucky boat, he would buy beer or coffee and some food for the old man's supper to keep up his strength to get the big fish they know he will catch tomorrow. Always Santiago insisted that he was not hungry, but the boy made him eat. And with his own bait he kept extra for the old man now. It was like an investment in his love and faith and sense of partnership. He only worried, now that it was September, how he could make enough to get Santiago some shoes and a new blanket and shirt and coat.

After supper, they read from the newspapers Santiago used to sleep on, read about the thing they loved most—next to fishing. What was it? Baseball.

They had seen the major league teams in Cuba for exhibition games and had fallen in love with baseball then. In special reverence they held the New York Yankees—and most especially old Santiago practically worshipped Joe DiMaggio. He was his hero, his knight in shining armor, for had not DiMaggio's father been a poor man and fisherman too?

When it was dark this night in September, the old man went to bed on his newspapers and the boy went home to his father's shack. In his dreams Santiago saw again the shores of Africa and the great lions he had seen there as a young man sailing a great ship. Then, as the old do, he awakened early, long before the dawn, and in the cold light of the fading moon, he went to wake up the boy who got their bait and helped him load the boat. Then they had their coffee, and the boy saw him off for the day's fishing.

This was the 85th day, and Santiago felt that it was a good one as he rowed out of the still dark harbor and straight out to sea, passing over what they called the great well that was 700 fathoms deep. He could hear the flying fish and soon it was light enough to see that he was farther out in the ocean than he had ever hoped to be this early.

One bait he let down at 40 fathoms, another at 75, another at 100, another 125. Each bait was a whole fish, a small tuna, and covered with fresh sardines on the points of the hooks.

The sun rose fast and high, and the sea became its mirror, a dark blue, almost purple mirror.

The old man sat and watched his lines and the life in the sea that he knew so well. He talked to himself quite a bit now about all he saw and thought. He had got into the habit of talking when Manolin was with him. He knew if anyone could hear him they would think him mad, but he was miles beyond any boat or person now, even the coastline was out of sight. He was alone and as he said—as long as he knew why and what he was talking about, that was all that mattered. Besides the rich people had radios to talk and keep them company. It would be nice to hear about the baseball games that way. But the business now was what he had been born to do—fish.

One line went down and he brought in a 10-pounder good for fresh bait.

Then the line that was down 100 fathoms pulled. Santiago held his breath. He knew exactly what was happening. Down in that world of the great deep 600 ft. below a marlin was nibbling the sardines. Delicately, knowingly, the old man's expert fingers held the line. Then with a sudden strike of lightning it went down and he felt such a weight of fish as he had never known before. Tensely he unrolled the first of his 2 great reserve coils of heavy line—enough for another 120 fathoms. Now he had to brace the line across his back. It hurt but there was no other way. If only the boy were with him. With all his heart he wished for Manolin —and that the fish would jump so that he could harpoon him.

But no, the fish headed out to sea towing Santiago and his

boat behind him. All afternoon they went like that and it was night and they were still going. The old man got their course from the stars and put all his strength into holding the line that was cutting his back, shoulders and hands. The last bird was gone before evening. It was all Santiago could do to get a drink from his water bottle. He had had no food and made himself eat some of the raw tuna he had caught for bait. To do that he had to free one hand. Then the other cramped over the line and was very painful. If only the boy were here to see and help in this great experience, for one could never tell it as it was happening.

The day's sweat chilled with the night on his body as he held on and they kept going, and it was morning again. It was incredible that there could be such a fish to climax the achievement of any man's life. Santiago began to feel a close sense of kinship with him as brothers linked together by this line between the top and bottom of the sea. He said the prayers he had been taught to say. He prayed the fish to jump so that he could see him, and at last he did and the old man could hardly believe his eyes, for it was at least 10 ft. longer than the boat.

Twice in his life Santiago had caught fish that weighed over 1000 pounds, but never alone. Here now was one over 1500 pounds and there was no one to help him and he was too old for such a fight. Or was he?

He called upon all his resource of strength and knowledge. The weaker he became, the more grimly determined. This was life or death for fish or for him. Against an opponent as noble as this, all his man's courage replaced his physical exhaustion and became strength.

Through bleeding hands he measured the line hour after hour all day again until incredibly it was night again. Then the power on that line changed and again he saw the mammoth marlin—close enough finally to aim his harpoon and the 2-day struggle was over.

Roping the boat to the giant fish all silver now in the water, Santiago got his sail up the mast to take them homeward. It would take many hours. Meanwhile there was rest. And he could look at the great beauty there beside him and see it as his fortune —at 30 cents a pound.

But neither danger nor struggle was over, for the scent of the fish was in the water and there were sharks hungry for food. They came all too soon, one after another. With his harpoon, then with his knife tied to an oar, Santiago killed all he could, but it was not enough and he had to see and hear and feel them tearing the meat off his great fish—destroying his prize.

And when in the dark of the night again he came into harbor, only the great skeleton of his fish was beside him and something hurt in his chest and he tasted blood in his mouth. The sharks had done this to him—not the great clean fight with the fish that was equal in dignity. No, it was the heartbreak of the sharks' destruction that would kill him now. It was all a mistake. He had gone too far out into the sea. It would have been better never to have caught and conquered the great fish than see this happen.

It was the boy who found him in his shack next morning. The men were all down looking at the boat and the skeleton of what the old man had accomplished. They had never seen anything like it. Nobody had. They were very proud of old Santiago. But the boy was crying. He always knew the old man could do it. But to do it—and then lose it. The author does not say so, but that was the day the boy became a man.

You will read this story with a tension you have seldom felt through words. You will learn a great deal of the sea—and man. There is great beauty in it—not of description but of spirit in action.

Is the meaning futility? Yes and no—and more no than yes, it seems to me.

It is true that as the saying goes—be careful what you want —you might get it. Sometimes when we go too far in our daring, what we get is too big for us and inevitably we lose it.

But what we remember here is that in a very simple way in a very simple man's life a great dream is realized and a magnificent courage is put to its full test. He won the crowning achievement in his life—and the fact that what he won was lost is only partly true. The experience and its record cannot be lost. They never can be when we justify ourselves and the faith that someone who loves us has in us.

What Hemingway said in "A Farewell to Arms" we can say even better of "The Old Man and the Sea"—"You are too brave to let them get you. Nothing ever happens to the brave."

The Nazarene

By Sholem Asch

November 1939

It is memorable that in this year of war clouds over Europe, clouds darkening our horizon with the nightmare of mass murder and madness, a great biographical and historical novel of the man known as the Prince of Peace comes to us. Some of us might even wish that it had been given that title,—but its author chose with wisdom and restraint a simpler one—"The Nazarene"—as he was called when he lived.

Sholem Asch is fifty-nine years old now, and almost thirty of those years have gone into the scholarship that made this book possible. It is the first of an epic trilogy which will include books on Paul and Mary and make evident the basic unity of our Jewish-Christian heritage of culture and civilization.

The critical acclaim greeting "The Nazarene" is tribute to the Sholem Asch art as historian in illuminating the shadows that too long have surrounded this story—presenting it at last not as a story of religion in the sense of any one religion, but as *history*. This is the value, the achievement. Almost all of us know something of the literature of our religions, but all too few of us know anything of their history. We know the story of the Nazarene, but not the history of the story—and from that history, the facts of time and place, we all have so much to learn—so much to fortify us against the evils of prejudice spawned by ignorance. Here now are the facts, as back across twenty centuries this historian, this literary anthropologist leads us into the world as it was then—the world of Rome and its dictator the Emperor Tiberius who had followed Augustus as Augustus had followed Caesar.

108

Tiberius had a step-daughter Claudia, a girl so degenerate that even none of the Romans would marry her. But to gain the favor of Tiberius, a Spaniard by the name of Pontius Pilate married her,—and as reward for this literally distinguished service, Tiberius appointed Pilate governor of the province of Judea.

We must bear in mind that in the world of that day, religion was pagan—the pagan gods and goddesses of Rome. Only one group of people were different. They were the descendants of some people who had come out of Egypt centuries before this, people called Jews or Hebrews. Now the distinctive thing about them was that they believed in only one God—and that to a man named Moses had been revealed His Ten Commandments for righteous living—and that some day there would come a Messiah who would deliver all the world from ignorance and evil, so that all men would live together in peace and brotherhood. This belief in one God and in the sacred books of the Torah which contained it,—this was the very life of these men and women. For this belief they were ridiculed and despised. But since Caesar's time it was Rome's policy not to interfere with their religion as long as they paid the heavy taxes and respected the supreme authority of Rome.

Besides there was something about that great Temple in Jerusalem and the fanatical devotion of these people to their belief that Rome feared—as man always fears what he does not understand. What Rome could not understand was how people could believe in a God you couldn't see—a God you couldn't make a statue of—an invisible power that meant more than the power of Rome. It was ridiculous; these people were mad. But the governorship of this province of Judea was a prize political plum, for the Jews would pay anything for their religious freedom, and the governors could extort as much money as they dared. And so to Jerusalem went Pontius Pilate and his lieutenant Cornelius with great expectations and plenty of soldiers to insure those expectations.

But the sight of Jerusalem itself was beyond any man's expectations. Dropped like a great white pearl between the hills, between the mountains of Moab, it was like a dream—this city

carved out of marble glistening in the brilliant burning sunlight—
the towers and domes of the places clustered like great white
grapes about the Temple. And the people were from everywhere
—Jews from Alexandria in rough woolen and sheepskin—Jews
from the deserts in camel hides and lion skins—Jews from Galilee
in simple sackcloth—Jews from Babylon and from the Rhine—
the streets of Jerusalem were a pageant—a rich riot of color.

And high up on on the gallery of their fortress, cooled by
oriental fans and parasols, drinking wine from the Cyprus and
eating the figs from Jericho, Pontius Pilate and Cornelius looked
down upon the Temple. In its great outer courts all the people
gathered, the rich and the poor—there the rabbis and the
scholars taught the moral law—and from this great court or
forum rose the marble steps leading up to the sanctuary itself—
a pyramid of white marble and solid gold.

Curiously, in the days that followed, Cornelius began explor-
ing the city—the marketplace with its fish and dates and figs and
olives and grapes without equal—the streets of the dyers, the
spice dealers, the goldsmiths, the tailors, and sandal makers, the
tent-makers, and the scribes forever writing with their goose-quill
pens making copies of the Ten Commandments. And Cornelius
went down into the lower city and, in contrast to the palaces with
their marble swimming pools and beautiful rose gardens, here he
saw the masses of the poor living in the most wretched poverty,
bled by the tax collectors, for in addition to the heavy taxes paid
Rome, there were taxes equally heavy for the Temple and the
High Priests. And he learned that next to Rome these people
hated the Priesthood, who no longer represented them, but Rome
—and who exploited their religion to grow rich and powerful
among themselves. It was not their High Priests but their rabbis
whom these people loved—men of their own class, self-dedicated
scholars and teachers. To the High Priests went their taxes, but
to the rabbis went their devotion. No fact is more important in
this story.

Between the High Priests and the Romans was a common
bond of mutual dependence to keep the mass of the people in
subjection. In the High Priest's house Cornelius felt at home—it
was so much like the Roman aristocracy. And it was there at a

banquet one night that he heard them discussing the rumor that there was a man in Galilee whom the peasants were claiming to be the Messiah. How they all laughed at this—those peasants and their idea of a Messiah—as if anything could come out of a place as poor as Galilee. But even as Cornelius laughed, he was thinking—thinking that if one day one of these Messiahs would really materialize—such a leader might deliver these people not only spiritually but—politically? Rome had better keep her eagle's eye on these so-called Messiahs—for that might be just another strange Hebrew word for—rebel. And so Cornelius confided his suspicions to Pilate—and continued to cultivate the company of the High Priest's young sons.

With them he got into the society that centered about the most famous woman in Jerusalem—Miriam of Migdal—or Mary Magdalene. A strange and fascinating woman of such beauty and brilliance that no man could resist her. She had many lovers— and they showered her with riches—and all this she gave to the poor with the same passion that she gave herself to her lovers. At her banquets honoring princes from Babylon and Antioch and Alexandria, she would appear from behind mists of incense, her body draped in her flame-red hair, and would dance to the erotic melody of her flute players and the chant of the Songs of Solomon. And immediately after such a night, she would go into seclusion for days to repent. It was as if this woman's body and soul made equal demands upon her, and she could not choose between them. And her lovers both feared and respected her, for she was like no other woman—or rather she was all woman and every woman—good and bad—mistress and mother of men.

Shortly after meeting Mary Magdalene, Cornelius was sent to Galilee to the court of Herod to iron out some difficulties between Pilate and Herod. And there in the palace and fortress of that fantastic voluptuary on the desert shore of the Dead Sea, Cornelius saw two sights he never was to forget. One was the prisoner Jochanan the Baptist, a man hardly more than a living skeleton chained in a dungeon cell. This man's crime was that he was a prophet who preached against Herod's Roman wife Herodias—and of the coming of the Messiah to deliver the people from all evil. Herodias hated him and wanted him killed. And

Cornelius quite agreed with her. But Herod had a strange fear of this man who did not fear him, and though he kept Jochanan in prison he refused to kill him.

And then one night at a banquet in honor of Cornelius, a little ten-year-old girl did what neither the Queen nor the Roman diplomat had been able to do. Her name was Salome and she was the daughter of Herodias by her first marriage to Herod's brother. Her child's body was already so developed that Herod's eyes, sated with the ripeness of the older woman, rested upon her with more and more depraved appreciation as she sat there beside her mother. And finally he waved away the other dancers and called upon Salome to dance for him. And this child could do what no person dared—she refused. Herod laughed and insisted and promised to give her anything she asked for if only she would dance for him tonight. At this her mother leaned over and whispered to the girl. And then Salome rose and came before Herod, stripped, and to the beating of a single drum by one of the slaves she began the dance of history. The beating of the drum reverberated in the blood of everyone in that banquet hall. Hypnotized they watched her—there was a fascination in the sight of this child using her body with all the knowledge of a woman. And when at last it was over, Salome reminded Herod of his promise and named her price—the head of Jochanan the Baptist. Herod's dark face flushed with wine and lust turned as white as death. Every eye was upon him as he hesitated in horror. And then the command was given—and on a silver platter the bleeding head of Jochanan the Baptist was brought in and presented to Salome—as Herod unable to stand the ghastly sight rose and left the table—and his wife smiled in triumph at Cornelius.

It was after this that Cornelius began hearing more and more about another prophet in Galilee—a young Rabbi—Yeshua ben Joseph—who was causing even more disturbance, because it seemed that whenever he appeared, the people would leave their work to gather around him and to listen to him. Even some of the Roman centurions were listening to him. And so Cornelius went to investigate this situation and to enforce discipline—and also partly out of curiosity to see if this man was really performing the miracles people said.

The Roman could never forget his first sight of this Jew. He found the young rabbi standing under a fig tree beside the harbor talking to the fishermen and farmers and carpenters and other laborers all grouped around him in complete absorption. As soon as Cornelius looked into those eyes, a feeling crept over him in spite of himself that here was no ordinary man. It was hard at first for Cornelius to understand everything he was saying, for he was speaking in Hebrew and Aramaic of course, but gradually the Roman could translate enough to get these words—"Blessed are the meek, for they shall have the Kingdom of Heaven"—"Blessed are the poor, for they shall inherit the earth"—"The day of the day laborer belongs to his master. But no one can be called master and lord, save the Lord of the world, and our days belong to him" . . .

At once Cornelius knew that he had not come too soon, for this was the kind of talk that would stir up labor trouble, unrest, and could lead to rebellion. This man was dangerous. He spoke with a peculiar power of authority which was dangerous. And unlike the other rabbis who confined their teaching and preaching to their own people, this man applied his words to everybody —Romans as well as Jews. In the name of religion he was sowing the seeds of revolt against the authority of the High Priests—and Rome.

And so Cornelius returned to Jerusalem and reported. The High Priest was inclined to ridicule the influence of this little rabbi in Galilee,—prophets were always appearing and disappearing—none of them should be taken too seriously—the best way to handle them was just to let them talk themselves out and ignore them. In short, why make something out of nothing? In theory Cornelius agreed, but only in theory, because indelibly impressed on his mind was the power of personality of Yeshua ben Joseph and his effect upon people.

He was right, for as the days of that springtime went by, the name and fame of Yeshua spread throughout the country like an ointment. His disciples numbered twelve now—twelve men who left their homes and families just to follow him and serve him. He led them from town to town and from village to village, visiting always among the poor to comfort them and among the ignorant to teach them.

Over and over he interpreted the truth that all men are brothers as the children of one Father—and that the only true sacrifice is the sacrifice of the spirit—and when the people asked him to explain the rigid severity and complexity of the laws of purity prescribed for them to observe, he told them very simply that to the pure in heart all things are pure,—that it is not what comes into a man from the outside which makes him pure, but what comes from within a man. And when the woman Mary Magdalene came to him and it was asked if she should be stoned as a harlot, he took her by the hand and called her "our sister" and said to the people "He who is without sin among you, let him cast the first stone."

Nothing that he said was new—he was speaking in the tradition of all the prophets before him—Hillel, Elijah, Elisha, Isaiah, Amos, Hosea,—the basis of all was in the books of the Torah—the Mosaic Laws. Indeed Yeshua himself said "I am not come to destroy the Torah nor the words of the prophets, but to fulfill them . . . Heaven and earth shall pass away before there shall be changed one jot or tittle of the Torah, and before all that is written therein shall be fulfilled."

But he was doing something new. He was simplifying these laws to and for the people. He was liberalizing and modernizing them,—and inevitably this aroused antagonism and resentment in certain groups.

Upon one man who doubted him, he turned his eyes in pity always—and that was his own disciple Judah of Kiriot, for Yeshua knew that this man's doubts sprang from the very excess of his desire to believe and to have his faith proved in fact. There was pity in Yeshua for such a man, because the very nature of faith is that it cannot and need not be proven in fact,—and so this man, as all men like him, must ever be in torment.

The question tormenting Judah's mind was—is Yeshua the Messiah so long awaited—or isn't he? This was the question that was being asked now everywhere.

Finally Yeshua led his disciples to Jerusalem, and wherever he appeared and preached, there followed endless discussion, arguments, controversy,—for he was speaking with an authority and daring like no other rabbi. Where did he get this authority? Was it authority—or blasphemy? Naturally men differed in their opinions, as men have always differed in their opinions about everything.

All winter the people of Jerusalem talked of little else, as incident followed incident. But when spring came again and the pilgrims began pouring into the city by the hundreds and thousands to celebrate the Passover festival which commemorates the deliverance from bondage in Egypt,—Pilate took action and ordered out the Roman guards. This Nazarene was a menace now. People were getting the idea that he was here to deliver them again as Moses had. He was attacking the High Priests, and the High Priests were afraid of his influence with the people,—for the people were already calling him their King—King of the Jews. That was enough for any Roman governor.

Pilate gave Cornelius the order to arrest the Nazarene— despite the fact that the court of the Sanhedrin could not be called into session on the eve of a holy day. If he was not brought to Pilate for trial, the High Priests would be suspected of conspiracy and the Roman soldiers would be ordered to massacre every Jew in Jerusalem. Such was the ultimatum.

Meanwhile the object of all this was in the poor home of a water-carrier. There Yeshua sat at a table with his disciples for the Seder supper service of the Passover, the supper which was to be his last.

The first man to leave that room that night was Judah of Kiriot. And it was he who ran to the High Priests and in hysteria made his offer to betray his rabbi—and to lead the Romans to the Nazarene. Why? Because only this will prove if he is the Messiah. If he is, a miracle will be performed to save him.

Cornelius was not interested in this fanatical reasoning. All that mattered was that this man or madman could be used. And so he led the soldiers through the silent streets while the people of Jerusalem slept—a cohort of five hundred men in armor to take one man a prisoner. They found him praying in a garden on the Mount of Olives, his disciples asleep on the ground. There they bound and led him back to the city.

All night the priests questioned and examined him, and in the morning he was taken to Pilate for trial. To Pilate the sight of this frail, pale man was a shock. Was this the powerful leader, the King of the Jews he had heard so much about? Then he heard the sound of shouts and cries of mobs outside the palace, as at last the people knew what had happened and was happening. It was time to show them who ruled Jerusalem—a rabbi or Rome. Abruptly he gave his order, a typically Roman order "Lash him—crucify him—crown him King of the Jews."

Vainly the great rabbi Nicodemon pleaded for a fair trial. Pilate's orders were already in effect. The Nazarene had been turned over to a company of German barbarians. His head was dripping blood from a crown of thorns—and on the cross laid on his back was inscribed in mockery the letters as Pilate had ordered—I N R I—the four letters always seen atop every crucifix, but seldom explained—I N R I, the first letters of the Latin words *Iesus Nazarenus Rex Iudaeorum* meaning Jesus of Nazareth, King of the Jews. In Latin the letter *i* is in place of our letter *j*.

Outside the walls of Jerusalem was the Hill of Golgotha where the victims of Roman justice were crucified—and there now was led this man who seemed to have become a symbol of all human suffering. On the summit of that hill they nailed the rabbi's body to the cross. But no sound came from him,—only the cry of people praying for a miracle—and the weeping of two women at his feet, his mother Miriam, Mary—and the other Mary, Miriam of Migdal.

And when at last a cry of anguish came from Yeshua's lips, Cornelius dipped a sponge in vinegar and raised it on a spear to his lips. Then the Nazarene spoke, as he looked down upon the laughing soldiers and said "Forgive them, Father, for they know not what they do."

Then like tears fell the words "Eli, Eli, lama sabachthani?— My God, my God, why hast Thou forsaken me?" And then with the last breath came the last words of every Jew "Hear oh Israel, the Lord our God, the Lord is One."

Thus ended the life of the Rabbi Yeshua ben Joseph—and began the life of Jesus the Christ as it was to endure in the minds and hearts of men inspired to the worship of the ideals his name represents—ideals of universal love and brotherhood which all of us have yet to make a reality on this earth, if we would not fail to keep faith with him—and with all those, before and since, who have lived and died for those ideals in the conviction of their truth —and the truth of their conviction.

The Nazarene

By Sholem Asch

April 1947

Ever since Sholem Asch's great work "The Nazarene" was published in the fall of 1939, it has always been a pleasure to me to be asked to review it and so continue to introduce it to an ever-widening circle of readers. Especially is that so at this time of the year—this time of eternal hope that comes with spring—this season so deeply significant to us all through the Christian Easter and the Jewish Passover.

Almost a lifetime of scholarship was distilled into the writing of this book, and that is its outstanding value—not as a story of religion in the sense of any one religion—but as a chapter out of history. Most of us know something of the literature of our various religions, but all too few know anything of their history. We know the story of the Nazarene, but not the history of the story.

From that history we all have so much to learn—so much to fortify us against the evil spawned by ignorance—as back across twenty centuries this historian, this literary anthropologist leads us to the world as it was then—the world of the Roman dictator, the Emperor Tiberius, who sent his son-in-law Pontius Pilate to Jerusalem as Governor of Judea.

At that time we must remember that religion was pagan—mainly the gods and goddesses of Roman mythology. Only one group of people were different, the people known as the Jews or Hebrews who had come out of Egypt. They were different because they believed that there is only one God. They believed that His Ten Commandments for right living had been revealed to a man named Moses who had led them out of slavery and to independence. They believed too that there was the promise that some day there would come upon this earth another leader, a Messiah to deliver the world from evil so that all men might live together in brotherhood and peace.

To the Romans this was ridiculous—to believe in a God you could not see and make a statue of, a God of no visible, tangible evidence. And yet there was something about that great temple in Jerusalem and the devotion of these people to their belief which Rome feared,—as men always fear what they do not understand.

In Jerusalem, as in every city ancient and modern unfortunately, there were more people who lived on the wrong side of the tracks than on the right side. And there among the masses of the poor, Pilate's lieutenant, Cornelius, learned that these people hated and despised their High Priests for having become nothing but Roman tax-collectors and politicians. The people were devoted only to their rabbis, the men who were their scholars and teachers—and that is a very important fact in this story.

That was why Cornelius was disturbed when he heard so much talk about a young rabbi down in Galilee who was said to be performing miracles and getting the people to believe that he might be the Messiah. A man like that could be dangerous to Rome, for that strange word "Messiah" could hold some Hebrew meaning of a leader for revolt and rebellion. And so Cornelius went to Galilee to investigate.

The young rabbi's name was Yeshua ben Joseph, and when the Roman officer heard him speak, the words were strange indeed—such words as "Blessed are the poor, for they shall inherit the earth"—"The day of the day laborer belongs to his master. But no one can be called master and lord, save the Lord of the world, and our days belong to Him." "Blessed are the meek, for they shall have the Kingdom of Heaven" . . . whatever that was. To Roman ears this was all the most radical kind of talk, subversive, sure to cause trouble, especially labor trouble.

Then he heard the rabbi deliver this prayer for the first time —"Our Father which art in Heaven, hallowed be Thy name. Thy Kingdom come. Thy will be done on earth as it is in Heaven. Give us this day our daily bread, and forgive us our sins as we forgive those who trespass against us. Lead us not into temptation and deliver us from evil." However translated, there was no acknowledgement of the power of Rome.

Cornelius stayed for some time in Galilee listening, observing and reporting to Pilate of the dangerous and increasing influence of this man who was leading his disciples from town to town teaching and preaching. Finally they came to Jerusalem itself.

Nothing in years had attracted so much attention and caused so much discussion and controversy. It was not what the Rabbi Yeshua said, for nothing that he said was new—he was speaking in the same tradition of all the prophets before him—of Hillel and Isaiah and Elijah and Hosea and Amos—but he was doing something new in the way he said it. He was simplifying the interpretation of all the ancient laws of their religion so as to take it out of the hands of the priests and heads of the scholars and put it directly into the hearts of the people.

Some thought that he had the right to do this—and others thought not—just as men have always differed in their opinions about everything. But entirely too many people were calling him Messiah and King—King of the Jews—and no Governor representing the Roman Emperor could let that go on and gather momentum. Not now especially with hundreds of pilgrims pouring into the city to celebrate the springtime festival of freedom, Passover, and getting the idea that Yeshua was here to deliver them from bondage again as Moses had from Egypt. With so much talk and feeling, anything could happen. Besides, there was pressure from the High Priests who resented this rabbi who challenged their authority. Pilate hesitated no longer and gave his order to arrest the Nazarene.

They could not find him at first, for he was in the poor home of a man nobody knew. There he sat with his disciples conducting the traditional Seder supper service of the Passover which was to be his last. One man left the table to betray him, as Yeshua knew he would—Judah of Kiriot. Always Yeshua had pitied this man for his doubts, for Judah was one of those persons who doubt from the very excess of their desire to believe—who must have their faith proved in fact—not knowing that the very nature of faith is that it cannot be proved in fact because it need not be. And so Judah, as all men like him, must ever live in torment and betray all that they love, as he did. And of course the question in his mind, as in so many others, was whether Yeshua was the Messiah or not. Now the way to prove it was to see if a miracle would be performed to save him.

And so that night while the people of Jerusalem were asleep, Cornelius led his cohort of five hundred Roman soldiers in full armor through the city streets to take one man a prisoner. It was time to end all argument and show these people that Rome ruled Jerusalem—and not a rabbi. And so Pilate gave his orders in typical Roman cruelty and contempt—"Lash him, crucify him, crown him King of the Jews!"

In vain the great Rabbi Nicodemon exerted every effort to plead for a fair trial. There wasn't a chance against charges of both treason and blasphemy.

Outside the walls of Jerusalem was the Hill of Golgotha where the victims of Roman justice were crucified. There now Cornelius led the man whose head was dripping blood from a crown, yes, but a crown of thorns—and who carried on his back a huge wooden cross inscribed with the four letters of the Latin alphabet, as Pilate had ordered—the four letters still seen atop every crucifix—I N R I—standing for *Iesus Nazarenus Rex Iudaeorum*—Jesus of Nazareth, King of the Jews.

And there on the summit of that hill, the scene of so much horror, they nailed the body of the rabbi to that cross. A symbol of all human suffering, at last a cry broke from his lips—and Cornelius as if in some final gesture of bravado raised a sponge dipped in vinegar on his spear to Yeshua's lips, as the soldiers laughed,—and the people wept.

Then the Nazarene spoke, as he twisted his body and looked down upon them and said "Forgive them, Father, for they know not what they do." And then like tears came those other words from him "Eli, Eli, lama sabachthani?—My God, my God, why hast Thou Forsaken me?" And at last with his last breath came the last word of every Jew—"Hear oh Israel, the Lord our God, the Lord is One."

And so ended the life of the Rabbi Yeshua ben Joseph—and

began the life of Jesus the Christ, as that life was to live on in the minds and hearts of men inspired to the worship of the ideals his name represents—the ideals of universal love and brotherhood which all of us have yet to make a reality on this earth—if we would not fail to keep faith with him—and with all those before and since, who have lived and died for those ideals in the truth of conviction—and the conviction of truth.

Hound-Dog Man

By Fred Gipson

March 1949

Every once in a while a writer is born who can write about the life he knows as naturally as biting into an apple—and you see and taste and smell and feel it all with him because it's just that real and just that perfectly communicated. The man who called himself Mark Twain could do it, which is why Tom Sawyer and Huck Finn are not just characters but the names of real fellows so true to the life of every man's memories and dreams that they go right on living.

And now Fred Gipson of Mason, Texas, has given us something of equally elemental simplicity and quality in a little book of less than 250 pages of sheer delight. Here is a talent to watch.

After three years at the University of Texas, Mr. Gipson went into newspaper work. But he kept wanting to go home to the hill country of Mason and hunt and fish again and write about the things a fellow sees and feels and thinks about in country like that—the things you learn only from mountains, trees, rivers, sunrise and sunset and a dog that loves you better than any man and longer than any woman. If he had been a Greek of Plato's Republic instead of a Texan today, he might have called these things "the eternal verities."

Back on the old Gipson farm with nothing but his courage, he borrowed enough money to fix up a house and then he went to work writing. That was 1940, and that year he made all of $150.00, he confides. But he kept at it and finally began selling enough magazine stories to support himself, a wife and two babies. In 1946 he wrote "Fabulous Empire," the biography of

123

Col. Jack Miller of the Miller Bros. 101 Ranch and Wild West Show. And now "Hound-Dog Man."

In this age of decadence it's a refreshingly rare and wonderful experience to get a breath of fresh air from a way of life as cleanly primitive and natural as the one this author knows and loves and has expressed so perfectly. This is the life that all life springs from and rests upon—the profound simplicity of nature as over against the society that man has made so complex that none of us can understand or enjoy it any more. It takes a hound-dog man to show this up and point the way back from the atom bomb to a good old coon hunt deep in the heart of Texas where a twelve-year-old boy like Cotton Kinney was getting ready to eat Christmas dinner.

Of course Cotton was not his real name but that's what his tow-head looked like, so that's what his father and mother called him.

Cotton was not one bit hungry for dinner and that's a bad sign in a twelve-year-old boy. But the reason was simple. This had been a most disappointing Christmas for him. He had wanted a hound-dog puppy and he did not get it. He had dreamed of it. He had even saved up all his cotton-picking money to buy Christmas presents for his father and mother—a dog collar and a lead chain and a cake pan big enough to feed a dog—and still no dog. How could a fellow ever grow up to be a man and go hunting without a dog?

No, Cotton had no appetite for Christmas dinner—not until he heard and saw Blackie Scantling's dogs coming down the road —and behind them Blackie himself—just in time for dinner.

Cotton's father was always glad to see Blackie but his mother was not. She considered him a definitely bad influence, especially on Cotton. For Blackie Scantling typified everything that we are taught not to do. He had never shouldered his responsibility to society. He had a good time and thoroughly enjoyed himself. He did not work when he could possibly get out of it. He was dangerously good-looking but did not bother about dressing up or getting married. He was a threat to every woman's sense of security because he made every man wish that he could do what Blackie did—and get away with it. He lived with his dogs in a house that was a comfortable disgrace and bachelor's paradise. He knew nothing about what was going on in Washington or Wall Street. But he knew where the coons and possums were and where all the foxes denned and where the wild turkeys roosted, and whose watermelons were getting ripe, and where the cat-fish were thickest and the squirrels filled the trees. What more important things were there for a man to know? School, according to Blackie, was pretty much a waste of time, for all that reading and writing were liable to ruin a boy's shooting eye. Cotton said amen to that and agreed with all his heart. Foot-loose and fancy-free, that was Blackie, and a dream come true. Why did Mama sniff at such wisdom and call it ignorance and laziness? And the way she failed to appreciate Blackie's dogs when they ran all over the place was just plain awful and downright embarrassing to a fellow.

Somehow Blackie always got off on the wrong foot with Mama. Like today. The way he praised her fried chicken and biscuits pleased her no end, especially when he compared them with a certain neighbor's whose biscuits "squat to raise and then bake on the squat." But then he went on and spoiled it all by saying he had not married because "you can't find a woman that'll put up with what a good hound dog will. You take a dog like one of mine here yonder. You can starve him half to death. You can run his feet off to the bone. You can get on a high lonesome drunk and kick him all over the place. But he's still your dog. Ready to lick your hand or warm your feet on a cold night. Now show me a woman that'll do the same."

No, Mrs. Kinney did not like that—nor did she like the way Mr. Kinney laughed at it. Still less did she like it when Cotton began begging to go hunting now with Blackie during this Christmas holiday from school and Mr. Kinney agreed to let him. After all he had been just about Cotton's age when he had gone on his first big coon hunt and it was something every boy dreamed of and every man remembered. As a matter of fact Mr. Kinney was dying to go again himself, but being Aaron Kinney and not Blackie Scantling he knew he had to stay home and work. Besides Blackie could be trusted to take care of the boys, for of course Cotton could not go without his bosom pal Spud Sessums.

Cotton was so excited he could hardly sleep that night waiting for morning to come to start off. His mother told him good-bye as if she never expected to see him alive again. His father let them take the horse and wagon and off they went to pick up Spud.

Spud was almost as tow-headed as Cotton and had just as many freckles. He was known for having the best melon-thumping ear in the county. No night was too dark for him to pick a ripe melon. But most wonderful of all to Cotton was that Spud had his own dog. Just a little black feist to be sure, but all his own—and that was what was important.

Cotton loved his mother but he could not understand why she would not let him have a dog. She said it made a fellow waste his time off in the woods hunting instead of going to school and church and working, but shucks, didn't she know you wasted just as much time dreaming about it?

Yes, it was a grand feeling to be away from women with Spud and Blackie and do just as you pleased, eating fresh fried squirrel and rabbit with your fingers and not bothering about washing your face and combing your hair.

It was a pretty exciting day with things happening you'd never forget. Like getting those squirrels and rabbits and the way Blackie almost caught an armadillo—and the way he put that old bull in his place that got after him. Yes sir, that was something to see and remember. That Blackie was some fellow—the way he went right into that charging bull and kicked and cussed him. Cotton and Spud had just sat there in the wagon with their eyes almost popping out at the sight.

The country itself gave you goose-bumps. It was so big and rough and wild and lonesome-like that it made you afraid and love it at the same time. Cotton felt as though nobody but God and Indians had ever been there before. Of course he knew better than that. He knew they were on Dave Wilson's ranch, but it just didn't seem possible to connect all this with any one man.

They had just set out their traps and pitched camp when Dave Wilson came along breaking in a new horse. Out riding with him was his young sister-in-law Dony Waller. And right away Cotton felt something happen to Blackie the minute he set eyes on that girl. He just wasn't the same Blackie after that and it made Cotton wish she hadn't come and changed things. There was a look in Blackie's eye that made Cotton feel in the way. He had seen that look in his father's eyes sometimes when he looked at his mother. And then Blackie and Dony began talking a kind of double-talk, saying one thing and meaning another like his father and mother did sometimes when they didn't want him to understand.

Dony was an awfully pretty girl—so pretty that Blackie said "a man ought to put her in a picture frame and keep it setting on his mantel-board just to look at." And even Cotton had to admit she rode her horse as well as any man. And she had a way of laughing that seemed to echo the way Blackie laughed at things. But Cotton was glad when she left so that Blackie could get his mind back on their coon hunting.

And that night when the moon rose big and white over the river and trees, they went on their hunt. Blackie's hounds picked up a trail in no time, letting out that deep roar that is half howl and makes your blood tingle with excitement and your hair stand on end. You could hear their baying for miles. The air shook with it.

It was a chase that wore them all out, but finally it ended at a big live-oak tree. Two pairs of eyes glistened down at them. Two coons instead of one. Not until then was it discovered that they had forgotten, of all things, to bring along the gun—but that didn't bother a man like Blackie. He just climbed up on the tree and shook down coon No. 1. Only trouble was that coon No. 1 turned out to be Spud's little feist dog. Then when the real coon came tumbling down, so did Blackie yelling to Cotton to hit it with his club—but instead Cotton missed the coon and hit Blackie. Off went the coon with Blackie racing after it right into the river where he killed it with his ax. Yes sir, that was some hunt—and the biggest boar coon they had ever seen.

The sun was rising when they got back to camp to eat and sleep. Then Dave Wilson came by to invite them to his house for supper and to tell about the coon hunt.

As they walked to the ranch house at sunset suddenly the air whistled with wild ducks with the last rays of sunlight making their feathers look like flames flying across the sky. It was all so beautiful it hurt. It hurt too to feel Blackie's disappointment when he saw that Dony Waller wasn't at Wilson's. And when Mrs. Wilson's cornbread and milk tasted so much like home, Cotton began feeling homesick for his mother all of a sudden.

But old Grandma and Grandpa Wilson made you forget almost everything—the stories Grandpa told and the way he could cuss and the way Grandma told him he was sure to go to Hell for it. Grandma dipped snuff and it sizzled like bacon when she spat into the fire. She just sat in a big rocking chair by the fire and wouldn't budge out of it. She said "I'll set and be waited on. I've done my work in this here world. For forty years I waited on a man and seven boys. Now I quit. I set down in this here chair and told 'em I was done. I'll set and rock till I draw my last breath." And when Blacke said how fine she looked she said "No, I'm mighty porely. It'll be the Almighty's mercy if I last to eat the greens come spring. Look at my hair—white as a snow bank. Blooming for the grave I am. Just an old woman a-setting in this rocking chair and blooming for the grave." Where-upon Grandpa said to Cotton and Spud, "Let this be a learning to you boys. Keep your freedom just as long as nature will permit. Don't never marry till you can't put it off no longer."

Going back to camp that night they caught a big wild turkey and Blackie said it was closer to go by Dony Waller's papa's house and take it to them to cook. Cotton and Spud knew right off that was just an excuse to see that girl again.

She didn't seem one bit surprised to see them, almost as if she'd been waiting for them. She was just as glad to see Blackie as he was to see her. Mrs. Waller was glad to see that big turkey. And Cotton saw a little coal black hound puppy that was a dream on 4 legs. Somebody had given it to Dony but it would not have anything to do with her or anybody else. It was a one-man dog that had not yet found the right man, they said. And then the most wonderful thing in the world happened as that puppy shyly, slowly but surely came up to Cotton and licked his hand. Cotton almost cried for joy. Like he did later that day when Dony's papa played the fiddle and the music said all the things Cotton had felt when he had seen the wild ducks flying.

Mr. Waller was a strange man. Folks called him a poet. He looked at Cotton and said "There's a time when a boy can lay his belly on the ground and feel the heartbeats of the earth coming up to him through the grass roots. That's his time to prowl. That's his time to smell the perfume of the wild flowers, to hear the wind singing wild in his ears, to hurt with the want of knowing what's on the yonder side of the next ridge. The Almighty, he never meant for a boy to miss them things when that time comes."

It was night again when they got back to camp to sleep. Later Cotton woke up hearing a sound like a long clear sweet bugle call coming nearer and nearer. Blackie said it was a hound dog on their trail. His dogs were answering it now too and their voices all blended in together but with that one so high above them like a woman singing. Then all of a sudden it was right there in Cotton's arms snuggling up to him and licking his face— the little black puppy that had followed him to say "I'm yours and you're mine forever" as only a dog can. Blackie said that was the smartest hound pup he'd ever seen. Cotton couldn't say a thing. He just prayed his mama would let him keep it.

Early in the morning Dave Wilson brought another horse out to break, but for once his luck failed him—he was thrown and broke his leg. Cotton got on his old mare and rode like the wind to town for old Dr. Cole.

Then they went racing back to the Wilson house where Blackie and Spud had managed to carry Dave home. The house and yard were already filling up with neighbor folks come to help. The women brought food and the men jugs of whiskey. Dr. Cole had the patient get good and drunk and swallowed half a bottle himself. Setting a broken leg was a job that called for plenty of alcohol for everybody concerned.

Cotton was never so happy to see anybody in his life as when his mother and father got there. And when his mother said he could keep the puppy—if he kept him out of her flower beds— Cotton was ready to go home. In fact his own home where people never got drunk and carried on as they were here now—that home was all he wanted to get back to and never get away from again—except to go hunting with his own hound-dog of course.

When Blackie married Dony Waller, Cotton couldn't keep

from crying. Somehow Blackie was lost now and would never be the same. There never would be another coon hunt with him like that again. He'd have to settle down and go to work and take care of his wife and be like all other men. Cotton's father seemed to understand why the boy was crying. He put his arm around him and said "Son, a man can't romp and prowl and play all his life. It ain't natural. There comes a growing up time when it's nothing but right for him to step between the traces and pull his part of the load."

I know of no book with a better valedictory to childhood than that,—do you?

The King and I

By Rodgers and Hammerstein

September 1951

Last March at the St. James Theater in New York a musical play opened with instantaneous success and ever since has been a sell-out for so many months ahead that getting to see "South Pacific" was a cinch compared to this. The show of course is "The King and I," as fine an example of theater as our stage has had in a long time. And to read as a play in book form, it's a delightfully rich and rewarding experience of comedy and drama.

In theater, both on stage and screen, I am often reminded of what I once heard a very fine cook say—that you can only get something good out of the pot if you put something good into it. Even great acting cannot make a fine play out of a poor story. That's why "The King and I" is so good—it grew out of a book that had something to it in originality and value.

When Margaret Landon wrote the book "Anna and the King of Siam" in 1944 and I reviewed it, I told how she had been on a trip to Siam some ten years before and came across a couple of books written in 1870 and 1872 by an Englishwoman named Anna Leonowens, books that told of her amazing experiences as teacher of the royal children of the King of Siam. These books had been suppressed and out of print for over fifty years. They were a real discovery and her story has now become something of a current classic, translated into all the major modern languages and Braille, and now the hit of Broadway with Gertrude Lawrence and Yul Brynner in parts for which they will always be remembered.

Anna Leonowens was the wife of an English army officer and

they lived in Bombay and then in Singapore where he died soon after the birth of their little boy. The young widow, highly educated herself and especially in Oriental languages, opened a school in Singapore and there she was engaged by the Siamese Consul to go to Bangkok. The King wanted to have his children taught English. This was the first time in history that an Oriental monarch had ever done such a thing—the first time a foreigner had ever been allowed, much less employed, inside the royal harem.

King Mongkut was a remarkable man, keenly intelligent and interested in science and highly educated himself. He had studied for the Buddhist priesthood before he became King. A bundle of contradictions, he had one foot in the past and the other in the future, a man of transition who clung to the antiquity of the East and yet reached out for the modernity of Western civilization. He knew that if his country was to survive in the face of British and French colonial expansion and the world of trade and commerce, he must bring his country and people up to date. Yet the old tradition of his training and the customs of centuries were not easily changed. The result of the conflict between his new interests and old loyalties and habits made the man an eccentric of split personality—delighting in his studies and his correspondence with Queen Victoria and Abraham Lincoln, while at the same time accepting the slavery of his subjects as a matter of course. He was an absolute tyrant—and a great liberal—a combination that resulted in some very amazing and amusing situations—especially with Anna Leonowens.

We meet her as the curtain rises on Act I of our play as Anna and her little son Louis are ready to get off the boat that has brought them to Bangkok. The lights of the city can be seen; the boat is ready to dock; the royal barge has come out to meet it with the King's Prime Minister.

Anna, a beautiful woman, is as excited as little Louis as they stand among all their luggage on the edge of this great adventure. The Captain of the boat is frankly worried about it all and warns Anna that a great deal will depend on the impression she makes on the Prime Minister.

Matters are not greatly helped when Louis sees that the men

on the barge are naked except for a few necklaces and belts with daggers in them. He runs to his mother and asks if she's afraid. Anna says "no" and that the way never to be afraid is to whistle.

And so she and Louis are whistling away as the Prime Minister comes on board, the whistling detracting somewhat from the dignity of his entrance preceded by guards and an interpreter he does not need, for when Little Louis says, "I don't like that man," the man assures them that he understands English—in perfect English.

He is to escort them to their apartments in the Royal Palace. Anna protests this, as her contract stipulated a separate home of their own. The Minister says His Majesty is too busy to bother about such details at present as the late Queen is being cremated with several weeks of ceremony. She died four years ago. So Anna can either accept the arrangements made for her or else. She accepts them—whistling.

The next scene is in the palace. The King is dictating to a secretary. He speaks very rapidly, frequently repeating himself and snapping his fingers for emphasis and to hurry things up. He has no time to waste—on anything. Time is his only enemy—with so much to be done. You feel the power—and the charm—of his personality. He pays little attention to the dancing girls trying to entertain him—and calls for the Prime Minister who introduces an emissary from the Prince of Burma who brings in a present for the King. The present is a very beautiful young girl —Tuptim, who has been taught to speak English. The King looks her over and accepts her as an addition to his harem. Tuptim is not too happy about it, for she has a sweetheart of her own.

When Anna is introduced to the King, she reminds him of his promise to give her a house of her own apart from the palace. The king recalls no such promise and is amazed that a woman dares argue with him. At once we see and feel the meeting of two characters of equally strong will power, and even as they clash, there is a respect for each other.

The thing that shocked Anna more than anything was the way everyone prostrated themselves on the floor or ground in the presence of the King. This was the custom and they were all used to it. But to Anna, this was something that she was going to do something about.

As if reading her mind, the King suddenly orders his head wife Lady Thiang to stand up as he introduces her to Anna and orders the royal children brought in to meet their new teacher. He has only 67—because, as he hastens to explain, he began very late. Obviously, he adores every one of them, and as they file in one by one—except the twins who come together of course—Anna falls in love with them all. More adorable boys and girls you can't imagine—and they are drawn to Anna immediately and can't keep away from her. Especially Crown Prince Chulalongkorn, son of Lady Thiang and heir to the throne—and just a little older than Anna's own Louis.

Then the King calls in all his favorite wives, for he wants Anna to teach them as well as their children. The wives are completely fascinated by Anna—especially her hoop-skirt dress which they can't resist lifting to peep under to see if she herself is really shaped like that! They are much relieved when she laughingly proves she is not.

One of the young women is already able to speak and read a little English—and the book she is most anxious for is the one she calls "The Small House of Uncle Thomas"—a variation of title that would have surely delighted Harriet Beecher Stowe.

As the play goes on we see what great success Anna has with her pupils—both the children and their mothers. They are all happy with each other, but Anna keeps reminding the King of his failure to keep his promise to let her have her own house and threatens to leave if she does not get it. He has never had his royal honor questioned before nor had anyone walk out on him—alive. And his stubborn pride is outraged. But Anna is just as proud and angry—but not quite so stubborn, for Lady Thiang finally prevails upon her to give His Majesty another chance, explaining how greatly he needs her, that . . .

> He is a man who thinks with his heart,
> And a heart is not always wise.
> He is a man who stumbles and falls,
> But this is a man who tries.

Anna agrees and goes to the King that night in his study

where he is reading through everything from the Bible to the latest New York newspaper reports on the Civil War. Between paragraphs he jumps up and paces the floor nervously. When Anna comes in we can almost feel his relief—even though he pretends that she has come to apologize and not to presume to help him, torn as he is between himself as man and King, as well as by the difference of East and West, the old world and the new.

When he finally told Anna that his agents had found letters written to London from Singapore calling him a barbarian and urging England to take over Siam as a protectorate, it makes her as angry as it has him. The English diplomat Sir Edward Ramsay is on his way to Siam now. Anna knows him from earlier in her life, and her idea, which she manages to let the King think is his idea, is that Sir Edward must be given the very best impression of the court here, so that he will report the truth at home to the Queen. And the way to do this is to dress the Siamese ladies in European fashion, entertain him with a splendid dinner party, dance, and theatrical performance—the play that Tuptim has written as her interpretation of "Uncle Tom's Cabin"—a version which I can only assure you is something out of this world.

The most hectic excitement follows as the King and Anna give orders and set to work day and night to sew the new dresses and get the ladies into them—plan the dinner and rehearse in a race against time as Sir Edward arrives ahead of schedule.

But somehow it all gets done, and Sir Edward is charmed— especially with seeing Anna again. And here for the first time we see the King show unmistakable signs of jealousy. He is greatly relieved when Sir Edward is gone—and then when he and Anna are alone and talking it all over, he orders her to teach him to dance as he saw her dancing with Sir Edward. They begin and as they dance, we begin to feel what they are feeling—a love they can never hope to express in any other way, a tenderly beautiful thing that must ever be a secret deep in each other's heart. In gratitude for all she has done for him and his country he gives her a magnificent ring—nor can she explain her hesitation in accepting it for the implication such a gift carries with it in our society.

Of course they quarrel again as is inevitable between persons of backgrounds as different as theirs, but the social differences are never as important as the common humanity we share together and which unites us—especially when we love. Always this is so, and as it is so between persons, it is so between peoples. Only the politicians keep us apart for their own purposes. All we ever need is just the chance to learn and get to know each other, as Anna said.

This is the all-important message of this perfectly delightful play—this and the beauty of a love story that forever stays a dream.

As the curtain falls on the last act, the King is dying. With him are all his wives and children—and Anna who not only has her house now but the joy of seeing that peculiarly great man understand and approve the way young Prince Chulalongkorn will rule as she has taught him—first of all to proclaim that no man or woman approach him on hands and knees but stand before him with head erect, with respect in their eyes instead of in their vertebrae.

Such was the great work accomplished by one teacher for a whole nation. If we only had more of them like Anna?

Our generation is concerned now and will be with aiding foreign countries, liberating them from oppression of many kinds. We need to learn that to teach is not to dominate. To teach is to open minds, not stuff them with our ideas. Every people have their own culture to develop, just as we have ours. The process of education is to break the chains of human bondage, not to forge new ones.

The Patton Papers, Volume 1

Edited By Martin Blumenson

February 1972

Outstanding in importance is a 960-page collection of "The Patton Papers," the private letters and diaries of the world-famous General George S. Patton Jr., perhaps our last great military hero. Presented and edited by Professor Martin Blumenson, the eminent military historian of the Naval War College in Newport, Rhode Island, this book is Volume 1, covering the years 1885–1940. Later it will be followed by a second volume to cover the General's private record from 1940–45, the last World War and his untimely death.

In 1903 the eighteen-year-old Patton wrote in a school paper at the Virginia Military Institute, "The character of Caesar, if a man so complex can be said to have a [single] character, is extremely difficult to define."

The same statement is true of him, which is why none of the many biographies of Patton, nor even the memorable screenplay starring George Scott, fully revealed this man who combined such contradictions as scholar and poet, soldier and philosopher. We knew and have seen him portrayed only as the swaggering, ruthless military leader who inspired extremes of love and hatred, the man who kept World War II from lasting longer and who, had politics and diplomacy given him free rein, would have ended it even sooner, minus a Berlin Wall and Iron Curtain.

How and why did he create the image of Blood and Guts, the image most feared by the enemy among all Allied commanders?

It *was* an image, a part played to the hilt for an effect to accomplish a purpose—the purpose of victory. But first of all he had to accomplish this within himself; he had to vanquish the

137

inner anguish of his own doubts, so that publicly and professionally he could personify positive and supreme confidence. If
he did not tolerate weakness in others it was because he would
not tolerate it in himself. The ego that the world saw was very
different from the private confession written to his daughter when
he was given the stars of a general: "I don't feel any different than
when I was second lieutenant except that perhaps I have less self-
confidence."

One quality that shaped the man was forever consistent:
compulsive ambition, the necessity to do his best—to excel, to
win whatever objective was to be won.

Few men's letters show such sensitivity of thought and
feeling about the standards and values inherited from his family
and his country. This was more than mere pride. Rather it was a
thought-out, reasoned-out awareness of responsibility to perform
and to achieve. In fact, these letters to the family he loved so
intensely and devotedly are not only a joy to read but a revelation
of personality and an almost Renaissance mind—a mind that set
out to inquire, to learn, to perfect its potential, whether the
subject be the classics of horsemanship or fencing or heavy
artillery. You lived and you fought one way: you attacked, and
you kept it up till the job was done. As he wrote once in his
student notebook at West Point, "If you have done your
damndest and failed, now you must do your damndest and win."
When this involved apple-polishing and acting a part, so be it,
but do it with grace, masculine grace.

He gathered his strength from the quiet things he loved—
reading and study, fishing, riding a fine horse in the country,
sailing a good boat. And certainly he liked to write, expressing in
letters his own sense of personal history. This was an art he
mastered, even though for the life of him he could never learn to
spell.

Nobody could have had a happier home life, as he was
keenly aware. Patton was born in San Gabriel, California, in
November 1885. His father was a lawyer whose family was Old
South aristocracy and his mother was from a wealthy pioneer
California family. Besides George Jr. they had one other child, a
daughter. Together they spent most of the summers on Catalina

Island. There was a good resort hotel in the little village of Avalon, and at the turn of the century the island was in all its primitive beauty with mountain goats on the cliffs and a paradise for swimming and boating. There in 1903 the seventeen-year-old Patton met sixteen-year-old Beatrice Ayer from Boston, heiress to an industrial fortune. For the boy and girl it was love at first sight and forever. They were married in 1910 after his graduation from West Point.

Some of Patton's most beautiful and interesting and, of course, revealing letters in his book were to Beatrice, for whenever they were apart he wrote her almost daily.

Other letters of special interest are the ones he wrote to her father and to his own father explaining his firm decision to follow a military career, his reasons and his philosophy of ambition. Later came his letters about his great friendship with General Pershing, their time together in the Southwest, and finally the full expression of his own genius in World War I when he made the Tank Corps a deciding factor for victory. Then there was the impatient waiting through another two decades for the fame of greater victory against greater odds in another World War when mobility and mechanization on the ground and in the air would give his coordinating skill the challenge he knew he could meet— because he must, because he was Patton.

You will meet him as he truly was in this book I so completely recommend to you—"The Patton Papers."

The Patton Papers, Volume 2

Edited By Martin Blumenson

October 1974

Now we have the book that completes the life story of General George S. Patton Jr.—the new and concluding volume of "The Patton Papers," edited and in part written by military historian Martin Blumenson. Many of you remember the first volume published two years ago which gave us the life of Patton as he grew up as man and soldier. This was done from his own private letters and diaries, and any biographical gaps were filled and written by Mr. Blumenson.

This unique and definitive combination of autobiography and biography is now carried forward and completed in the second volume that covers Patton's life during the war years, 1940–1945, when he rose to his fame as perhaps our greatest combat commander and general, then experienced a sense of failure and personal frustration before the accident that caused his death in 1945.

It would seem that he died at the right time, for he could never have adjusted to what happened later. Any consideration of amnesty would have been incredible to him. Fighting wars and not winning them with decisive victories would have been incredible to him. Political negotiations were farcical to him. He saw the United Nations as a vast hypocrisy. He had learned his most basic lessons from General Pershing, who hated allies. Eisenhower, as this author-editor points out, was brought up in the same school, but outgrew it.

Like Pershing, Patton was a cavalry man and he transferred cavalry techniques to the Tank Corps, using tanks as if they were

140

mechanized horses for constant mobility. I need not tell you how dramatic were his victories when and where they were needed most—in Africa, in Sicily, in Europe. As he told his men, "God have mercy on our enemies. They will need it."

The dash and flair of the cavalry man never left him. Once when he was to preside at a ceremony opening a new bridge, and they gave him scissors to cut the ribbon, he threw them away with the words, "I am not a tailor. Bring me a saber." Someone did, and he sliced the ribbon in style.

Another time he was ordered to bypass a city because it was thought that it would require four divisions to go through it. His answer was, "I have already taken it with two divisions. Do you want me to give it back?"

This was the combat genius that made his leadership invincible—a spirit he could and did project to all the men of his Third Army. He demanded the impossible but he shared it with them, every step of the way, as no other general did.

His was the genius of the fighter, and when the fighting was over, so was he. This was his destiny, as he knew. But he was too complex a man to readjust himself. He was torn by too many inner conflicts of psyche, and this is the great interest in his revelations about himself in these private papers.

He was a scholar in classic literature and history, but with enormous gaps of ignorance. He had monstrous prejudices which were self-destructive. He was born to lead but unfit to govern. He was George Patton, and now we know the thoughts and feelings which he usually concealed and which fed his ego and made him succeed as a general and fail as a man in the goals he held paramount. All this is revealed in this book of self-portraiture with complete honesty.

My Name Is Asher Lev

By Chaim Potok

April 1972

A superlative writing performance has just come to us in a new novel entitled "My Name Is Asher Lev." The author is Chaim Potok who won many awards for his great 1967 novel called "The Chosen," followed two years later by "The Promise."

The most amazing thing about those novels of such outstanding literary quality was that they became bestsellers. Not that really good books do not become bestsellers—they can and they do. But Rabbi Potok was writing about a tiny group of people in Brooklyn who are completely foreign to most of us: the highly orthodox Hasidic Jews. Yet the beauty of their faith and the problems it posed for their children today came through to us as clearly as the reality of our next-door neighbors. They were never strangers to us.

This is the magical gift of Chaim Potok—perfect communication, profundity never lost in profundity.

Now in his new novel, "My Name Is Asher Lev," he accomplishes even more. Again we have a family in that little society of Hasidic Judaism in Brooklyn, but not only do we have depth of devotion among father and mother and son, we have the generation gap and, much more than that, the gap which forever separates the compulsive creative genius from the rest of all mankind. To do all this as simply and clearly as ABC, while still assuming an always intelligent reader whose heart and mind are open to be touched and stirred—this is the work of a master with words.

The only character study of a creative artist at all comparable is the classic of 1910, Romain Rolland's "Jean Chris-tophe," and that took three volumes originally to do what Potok has presented in less than 400 pages.

Asher Lev begins telling us his story as he lived it, for he is trying to explain how it happened that he is now the famous and infamous Asher Lev, the center of so much controversy in today's world of modern art, another Chagall, another Picasso—yet always himself, Asher Lev—and why, too, he is the center of so much controversy among both Jews and Christians.

It began as a mystery, as every baby born is a mystery as to what it will be and become. This boy was born in Brooklyn in 1943 to a young husband and wife who knew their family traditions back to the fourteenth century in eastern Europe, families of rabbis and scholars who lived by their faith and survived by it. When the Hasidic Movement began in the eighteenth century to preserve those vital traditions and stories for people deprived of them by persecution, especially in Russia, the families of Asher's mother and father were part of it.

Now in America, Asher's father worked for their leader, the great Rabbi in Brooklyn who sent him to government officials in Washington and Ottawa to seek help for Russian Jews escaping to freedom, one by one. Naturally, he expected his son to follow in his footsteps.

But at the age of four, little Asher began reaching for any kind of pencil or pen or chalk or crayon to draw pictures: pictures of everything he saw in their little apartment and out of the windows, on the street, at the synagogue, or in the park with his mother. At first they thought it was just a normal, childish expression and pastime.. But when he went to school, he did not study. All he did was draw and sketch, and his father became impatient with him, for many serious things were on his mind—his work to save lives and his people's heritage, then the serious illness of his wife. To have his son wasting time drawing pictures was too much.

But Asher could not stop his hands from drawing. He would leave school and go to the museum and copy pictures. Once he even stole some paints and brushes—until his mother bought him some.

More and more she was torn between her love of husband and son, understanding the conflict between them. It grew worse when her husband was sent to Vienna to carry on his work in Europe, and young Asher would not go. She stayed with the boy.

Finally it took the wisdom of the Rabbi to intervene. He saw some of Asher's pictures, saw the talent which was driving him and arranged a meeting with the great New York painter and sculptor Jacob Kahn, who was so impressed with Asher's work that he agreed to teach him what he had not already taught himself. Then Mrs. Lev went to Vienna to join her husband.

Asher was alone now in the world of his commitment, the world of art—a world with its own traditions, a world which recognizes no boundaries between people and what they believe.

He worked day and night, his inner eye seeing pictures faster than his hands could paint them. He had to have his freedom, yet he missed all he had loved so deeply at home. He knew that there can be love without understanding, and that one must accept this as the price of the artist's freedom.

His parents returned home, and he had his first exhibition, a very successful one. Asher Lev was on his way, but it was a way he had to walk alone.

He went then to Italy and Paris, and it was in Paris that he painted the masterpiece which was to catapult him into fame and controversy: the great oil painting called *Brooklyn Crucifixion,* a picture of his mother in the frame of their window at home. She was standing as he had so often seen her, waiting and looking for husband or son or both, praying for a safe return. But in this picture he put his father on one side and himself on the other so that her torment of anxiety formed a cross between them, as indeed the heart of woman is in the love of wife and mother when husband and son are of equal strength, and their strength leads them in different directions, each true to himself and the gift God gave him.

I cannot recommend this novel too highly. To read "My Name Is Asher Lev" is to enrich yourself.

Roots

By Alex Haley
February 1977

There have been books that have exerted such influence and impact on society that they have changed our lives. Two outstanding examples here in America in the latter half of this century are Rachel Carson's "Silent Spring," which sounded the vital alarm in 1962 to protect our environment in the world of nature —and then the book that came to us in 1976 which recalled and stressed, perhaps even defined, the power of personal and racial heritage—Alex Haley's "Roots."

Dr. Haley is a man who had to find himself by finding out where he and his black American family came from—not only *where*, but *when* and *what* and *who* and *how*. That urge and search for source, for origin, for meaningful identity became compulsive, obsessive. No hardship or frustration was too severe to keep him from his research—twelve long years of it. The result is a book of just under 600 pages of fascinating narrative documentary—a saga of people, a story of men and women and their children, an epic of what and how they endured and achieved.

It's a proud, dramatic history and we begin it in the spring of 1750 in a West African village when a young father joyfully performs the ancient tribal ritual of lifting his baby son toward the moon and stars to proclaim his name—Kunta Kinte, the name of the grandfather who had come from Mauritania to The Gambia.

From then on we live in this child's world as he grows into boyhood and teen-age young manhood. It was a world he was to remember all his life—memories that would sustain him through the horrors of his capture by the slave-hunters and traders when he was brought to America. Then came the long years of

adjustment to existence as a slave under the brutality of plantation overseers; the learning of new language, food, customs; and
the rigid boundaries to a man's impulses and hope.

Don't jump to the conclusion that you have read and heard
all this before. You haven't. Not like this, for in these pages the
focus is different. Because of the novel form and the author's own
insights the personality, the thinking, and feeling of the individ-
uals become living reality. We are not spectators.

We share the therapy of love when at last it comes into
Kunta's life and then the love for his daughter Kizzy—the
ignominy of helplessness when she is sold and raped—and then
the rich vitality of her son Chicken George and the new freedom
of choice and sense of direction in his son—and finally the birth
of the baby who will be the son of a Cornell University professor
and the author of this monumental black classic in American
literature.

All of this is written and told not from the outside but from
the inside, the human inside—written and told with passion, yes,
but not with hatred, not with venom for vengeance. The past is
the way it was, no better and no worse than it has been for all
people who have been victimized by man's inhumanity to man.

What matters are the traditons, as Tevye sang in the folk
opera "Fiddler on the Roof"—the symbols of continuity from
mother and father to daughter and son of what life means to
them, the strength that comes from roots.

Don't rely on what television did and didn't do with this
book. It was not as lucky in receiving a totally faithful production
as was Ernest Gaines' "The Autiobiography of Miss Jane
Pittman."

Go to the book itself—"Roots."

Sacajawea

By Anna Lee Waldo

September 1979

Except to historians of the American West, and not to all of them, Sacajawea has too long been an unsung heroine, the first fully dimensional great American woman, so much more validly so than the better known Pocahontas. In fact, without Sacajawea's aid as interpreter and her knowledge of terrain, survival foods, and therapy, Lewis and Clark would have had more obstacles in their expedition's path than even the Continental Divide.

Anna Lee Waldo of St. Louis, who was born and grew up in Montana close to the Glacier Park wilderness whose lore and legends led her into years of research, has given us the monumental biographical novel we have needed. She has also put herself in the vanguard of today's trend of authors preferring original publication in paperback for her 1350-page story of the woman who linked the Indian's and the white man's worlds.

Perhaps we forget that if the Lewis and Clark military expedition had not been successful in finding out just what lay between the Missouri River and Pacific Ocean, President Thomas Jefferson's Louisiana Purchase would not be our western United States now. If Lewis and Clark and Sacajawea had not found a way across the Rockies to the Columbia River and Pacific coast and survived that two-year ordeal of thousands of miles, the French and British would have had it, and we would have lost over half a continent of our richest natural resources.

So much for history. Now for the woman, Sacajawea.

Her name is Grass Child when we first meet her with her father, Chief No Retreat, in the camp of their family and Shoshoni tribe, the People as they call themselves. The camp is in the Big Horn Mountains of what is now Wyoming, and she is a child of only eight or nine summers. The Indians did not count years as we do. They counted summers. No difference at all.

It's a loving family, her mother and father, her older sister and brothers and old grandmother. Grass Child is a girl who asks many questions, many more than usual for an Indian girl who was supposed to be quiet and listen to the men. But her father did not mind her questions. He only wished he knew all the answers.

It was not easy to lead his People and know what was best for them. Now in the Season of Gathering Nuts, which we call fall, the buffalo were gone and it was time to move camp and follow them for food before the Moons of Howling Winds and Snow arrived, when there would be hunger and the warriors too weak to fight off other tribes trying to steal the horses.

Would it be better to break tradition and change their tribal ways like those who gathered grass seeds and pounded and boiled them into flour with bear grease and water to make into flat cakes when there was no meat? Already his own squaw was beginning to do that, and it was good food. To reward her he gave her a beautiful sky-blue stone he had once taken from an enemy warrior. Into it he bored a hole and strung a thong of hide, and she wore it around her neck as her dearest treasure. We know it as turquoise.

Theirs was an unusual family. Grass Child's mother wanted no other squaw to help her in her work, though Indian women did all the work except the hunting and fighting. Nor did Chief No Retreat want another woman.

It was a happy home life for Grass Child until the day came to move camp for winter. The old grandmother whom she loved so much for all she had taught her must be told farewell and left behind in her tepee, alone. There was no choice. The tribe must move, and the old woman had come to her dying time and wanted them gone.

Into the old woman's hands her daughter put the blue stone, but after they were gone two days Grass Child ran back over the trail alone to perform the last ritual for the dead body of her grandmother and to retrieve the precious blue stone.

It was a harrowing ordeal for the girl but just the beginning of the testing of her courage and survival power, for on return to the tribe's new camp there came an attack by the Minnetarees and she saw her father killed and her mother scalped, and she herself was captured as a slave. Taken to their camp on the upper Missouri near the Canadian border, she had to recover from shock and sickness, learn a new tribal language and customs and to endure, young as she was, her first sexual experience.

But there were squaws who were kind, especially one who saw a spirit in her that was to give her a new name—Bird Woman —Sacajawea.

A name was most important to an Indian. It had meaning and was rarely to be spoken and never lightly. The girl was proud of her new name. It stood for her new life—much of which she hated, but she knew that what she was learning would bear fruit in the future—and she never doubted that future.

Then she was traded into another tribe, and again there was much to endure, but also more to learn, as we learn with her.

When she was taken to a fur traders' fair, she saw her first white men—men with hair on their faces, arms, shoulders, legs, chests, not just on their heads like Indian men. The white men's hair could be yellow as corn, and some had blue eyes. They had bottles of drink that made the chiefs act foolish and quarrelsome.

Ugliest of all was the fur trapper Charbonneau. He spoke the Mandan and Minnetaree tribal languages and two others Saca-jawea had never heard before—they were French and English.

Toussant Charbonneau was forty-three when this thirteen-year-old girl felt his eyes lusting after her. He was short, stocky and smelled of beaver and rum. The other men laughed and called him Squaw Man because he had many squaws as young as he could trade for them. A blustering bully, he had come from Montreal, his father French, his mother Sioux Indian, and he lived in the Indian villages trapping beaver and guiding and interpreting for other trappers and traders.

Such was the man who won Sacajawea in a game of chance that the men played. He took her to his lodge with his other two squaws, and so began another new life for the girl. At least there was food and plenty of skins to make into new moccasins and tunics with that cherished blue stone on its thong always at her neck—the last tangible touch of her family.

Then she was to be a mother, but not before the great day in that fall of 1804 when the Indian villages along the river went wild with excitement as they saw the boats of Capt. Meriwether Lewis and William Clark poling up the Missouri. Among all those white men was a most amazing sight: an all-black man—not painted black as the Indians first thought, but black skin, a black that did not rub off when the chiefs got to touch him. This was Ben York from Clark's family plantation in Virginia.

There were many guns on the boats, and the men all wore blue coats and carried pieces of cloth they called flags—red, white and blue—which they gave to the chiefs with sign language indicating that they came in peace. Then they built a winter camp and explained through interpreters that far to the east was a place called Washington where lived a Great White Father who wanted all the Indian tribes to live in peace. The chiefs listened, but they knew that this was foolishness, for how did you live in peace with those who stole your horses and women and children?

Most attentive of all was Sacajawea. Capt. Clark's red hair and York's blackness fascinated her, and she saw and felt their kindness. When Charbonneau asked to be engaged as interpreter, and Lewis and Clark learned that Sacajawea was a Shoshoni, they asked to talk with her, for when the snow and ice melted they wanted to go westward into Shoshoni land. Could she guide and interpret for them to find a way, a waterway through the mountains?

Overwhelmed by all this attention, plus by the chance of returning at last to her People, she began describing the country and soon became at ease with these men. They were impressed with her information and keen intelligence. As a result they hired Charbonneau in order to get her. But by spring she would have had the baby. Who ever heard of taking a woman and baby on such an expedition?

It was Clark who pointed out that this would show the Indians along the way that they came in peace and that her woman's knowledge could be helpful in caring for the men.

On a freezing February day, the young Sacajawea joined that mystery ritual of all women of all races who go down into the depths of pain to create new life—and it was York who helped her most of all. The baby was a boy, and she named him Pompy, meaning firstborn. Charbonneau named him Jean Baptiste.

As recorded in their journals and diary, it was April 7, 1805, when Lewis and Clark had their boats put on the river—the pirogues and canoes built during the winter—and the farewell speech was made.

And so began a year of experiences and adventure now brought to life in this novel as never before, for this is narrative history of the almost daily drama that this young woman, a baby on her back, shared with those forty-five men. Now in these pages we can share the reality of those months of danger and hardship and also her great happiness—the beauty of her Shining Mountains, their snowy peaks glistening white against blue sky—the rivers and falls and rapids—the vast open country where someday a nation would plant and harvest its wheat and ranch its cattle and set off gigantic parks for us to see the wonders of wilderness today—the joy of reunion with what was left of her family. Then comes the stabbing realization that no longer is she part of them but rather a link between them and these white men and black man whom she trusts—most of all Capt. Clark, so good to her and the baby, the man who teaches her that in his world a woman has a choice about the feeling in her heart. For the first time Sacajawea is in love, but she knows that what she and he feel for each other is never to be spoken in any of their languages.

After reaching the Columbia River and then the Pacific Ocean and surviving a winter of near starvation, they began the return trip the next year. Nobody had ever expected to see them back again, but there had been only one death, and John Coulter had left them to discover and explore what we know as Yellowstone.

For Sacajawea's sake Clark offered Charbonneau land to farm at St. Louis, the trading post for all the Americans, French and Indians who came up and down the river. Not only did Clark provide for Sacajawea, but he offered to take her son and the son of Charbonneau's other squaw and send them to school and college.

Lewis was made governor of the Louisiana Territory, but in

1809 at the age of only thirty-five he died on one of his journeys from Washington to St. Louis; it could have been murder or suicide.

In that same year Clark, governor of the Missouri Territory, married his Virginia sweetheart, Judy Hancock, who shared his friendship with Sacajawea completely.

Sacajawea was at home in the white world. Her son was safe with General Clark, and she came to a decision that broke every tradition for a squaw. No longer would she endure the brutality of Charbonneau. She left him and went alone into the southwest country of the Comanches, the land we know now as Oklahoma and Texas.

She was near starvation when she was found by a Comanche hunter whose name was Jerk Meat. He took her home to his village to live with his parents, sister and grandfather. They were good to her, and she recovered her strength and learned their language and Spanish to add to her many tribal tongues and French and English.

Gradually she overcame her yearning for her son, and despite her thirty summers she felt like a young girl in her love for this Comanche who was the counterpart of Clark. No more beautiful description of a marriage and mating can be found anywhere than in this part of the Sacajawea story. But the jealousy aroused in other women in the camp became a great danger to her.

From the east came the Americans and from the south came the Mexicans. Always there was fighting and the loss of land and buffalo. When Jerk Meat was killed, her life with the Comanches was over. Alone again she wandered northward in search of her son among the forts and trading posts, hearing of his success but always missing him by a few days or weeks or months.

With age upon her shoulders she had become a living legend in both the Indian and white worlds with her great knowledge of the best and the worst in each.

Into 1884 Sacajawea watched what was called Progress. She watched what it did to the land and to the people until she put up her last tepee. Then she lay down upon her last buffalo robe and gave her sky-blue stone of turquoise to a great-grandson in his jeans and cowboy boots to give to his bride. With it went a century of memories and dreams which are our history.

Agatha Christie

An Autobiography

November 1977

On January 12, 1976, a great lady and the most successful author in literary history, except for Louis L'Amour, died. Agatha Christie Mallowan was eight-five years old, a Dame of the British Commonwealth, master of the detective mystery genre, author of 88 books, 65 novels, 100 short stories, 17 plays—over 400 million copies in 103 countries.

Ten years before she had finished the autobiography that has come to us now, though she considered autobiography " . . . too grand a word . . . rather a journey not back through the past, but forward through memories . . . remembering what I want to remember . . . the ridiculous things that make sense . . . at seventy-five it is time to stop because this is all there is to say: Thank God for my good life and for all the love that has been given to me . . . I like living. I have sometimes been wildly despairing, acutely miserable, racked with sorrow, but knowing always that to be alive is grand. To be part of something one does not in the least understand is, I think, one of the most intriguing things about life . . . "

That gives you a sample of what you will enjoy in this 519-page visit with the remarkable woman who so completely satisfied the world of readers who delight in quality suspense. This reviewer was lucky enough to have a personal visit with her when she came to Dallas with her noted archaeologist husband, Max Mallowan, on his lecture tour. Her main concern was to hide her fame and try to remain incognito, not an easy thing to do. She was shy, and her feet hurt from her excessive weight. She wore tennis shoes under her long dinner dress, and when I suggested that she take them off, she was as grateful as if I had given her the Nobel.

That same naturalness is in this book which she began writing while on a dig with Sir Max at Nimrud, Iraq in 1950. She finished it in 1965. Utterly without temperament, she could write anywhere, whether in a room or under a tree or a tent in the desert. All she ever needed was a table.

She was born in 1891 at Torquay on the south coast of England, her mother English, her father American, and his main characteristic was "being agreeable." But the mother was a character, strong in personality and enjoyably changing her religion from Catholic all the way to Unitarian and back to Church of England. She believed that anything is possible and was largely responsible for Agatha becoming a writer.

At the very beginning Agatha Christie says "One of the luckiest things that can happen is to have a happy childhood." She did. It was a happy home of parents and children. Her first and most memorable gift was a dog. At five she was reading, and then her father taught her to write and figure. She was eleven when he died and the family life changed.

Private school in Paris came next and her love for music—both piano and singing, but she learned that she was not good enough to be professional. There was a winter of society life in Cairo, much popularity and many proposals, but Agatha returned home intact. She was writing some poetry and reading. D.H. Lawrence and her favorite, May Sinclair, whose novels she thinks should be re-issued now.

It was her mother who urged her to write a story as therapy to recover from an influenza attack. Then her sister Madge, who was a Sherlock Holmes addict, dared her to try to write a detective story, and Agatha began to think about it. But at a dance she met Archie Christie of the Royal Air Force and they fell in love. That was 1912. The war came and she went into nursing, and it was while she was working in the hospital that she began to plan her first detective story and created the Belgian refugee character Hercule Poirot. A publisher rejected it. She sent it to another and forgot about it.

On Archie's first leave at home they married, and when he returned and the war was over a baby girl was born, Rosalind. Then came the letter from the publisher—after two years they

had decided to take her book *The Mysterious Affair at Styles.*
Suddenly she was an author. They also cheated her on the
contract. As she says "I was a complete amateur. For me writing
was just fun."

Very soon it became more than that, as popular response
and demand called for more books, more stories, serial rights,
translations.

With an agent then to protect her success, Agatha Christie
was established. Everything was going wonderfully well—Archie
had a good job—they had a country house. But then her mother
died and Agatha became ill. To all that was added the shock of
her husband's infidelity and demand for divorce.

She passes over this miserable period in her life and reveals
nothing of her own mysterious disappearance for days. That was
something to be suffered and dismissed with recovery—and
recovery was in getting back to work and writing.

It was on a trip to the Middle East that she fell in love with
archaeology and Max Mallowan. He followed her back to Devon
and proposed. She tried to resist because she was thirteen years
older than he, but in later years after their wonderfully happy
marriage she said that it's fine for an archaeologist's wife to be
older because the older she gets the more interested he becomes.

The book glows with her human warmth and sincerity—and
her commentaries hold a treasury of wisdom that you want to
mark and reread. As with her play *The Mousetrap*, which has
broken all records for continuous performance for twenty-nine
years in London, there's an endless appeal for us in the style and
technique she mastered and made her own in book after book.

Now this one about herself keeps her with us as a person.